this way >>>

fairy

fairy

kirby

Palimpsest Press
1171 Eastlawn Ave.
Windsor, Ontario. N8S 3J1
www.palimpsestpress.ca

Printed and bound in Canada
Cover design and typesetting by Ellie Hastings
Edited by Jim Johnstone
Opposite title page photo: Don Pyle
Interior cover art: Philip Hare

Palimpsest Press would like to thank the Canada Council for the Arts and the Ontario Arts Council for their support of our publishing program. We also acknowledge the assistance of the Government of Ontario through the Ontario Book Publishing Tax Credit.

LIBRARY AND ARCHIVES CANADA CATALOGUING IN PUBLICATION

TITLE: Fairy / Kirby.
NAMES: Kirby, author.
IDENTIFIERS: Canadiana (print) 20260236500
Canadiana (ebook) 20260236519
ISBN 9781997508236 (SOFTCOVER)
ISBN 9781997508243 (EPUB)
SUBJECTS: LCSH: Kirby. | LCSH: Sexual minorities. | LCSH: Gay culture. | LCSH: Homosexuality. | LCGFT: Essays. | LCGFT: Anecdotes.

CLASSIFICATION: LCC PS8621.I72 F35 2026 | DDC C814/.6—DC23

there in the wet room tiled like an abattoir
these boys opened their towels like velvet curtains
    at an opera house
and I opened my mouth to sing

— Richard Scott,
"other people's dreams are boring"

My survival does not make me exceptional.
Luck, baby. History tells me I'll always be
a target. An orange rose in queer season.
Fairy knows where when to take cover,
fuck in the shadows. Dance in the night
of day. It's been this way, centuries sea to
shining limbs on the pier bathed in beauteous
chests eyes hearts cocks afoot aflame.
This is the place. Now the time pink ponies
reign underground, surface only to fill
lungs deep plunge low lower lower
rise rise again again this last night eternity.

17 May 2025, Queen Vickie Day

How noticeably quiet streets are long weekends in the city light rain taps the metal ledge off my balcony, a waft of deep purple lilacs below reach. Waken.

Where were we?

A boy, drenched in lilac groves, huge on a hill overlooking fields of soy and corn, white, purple, deep purple, variegated with white tips alongside a single dogwood resplendent.

Crabapple in blossom, as well as the pear, sister apple trees and mulberry. Patches of wild asparagus they were careful to mow around. The triumphant return of lightning bugs at dusk, a streetlamp in the drive beside an enormous erect pine that housed a bat swooping mouth open for bug clusters dancing in the light. Our tailless Irish setter sprints down the hill and back, again, again. “Here Lady!” A symphony of crickets, cicadas, friends playing tag, hide-and-go-seek made up games in adjacent fields, the smell of charcoal grilling meats, ballgame on the radio. Stars. Maps. Orion’s belt. Venus. Madame de la Luna.

Mine is the Fairy of Delicates.

Forget-me-nots. Lily of the valley. Lilacs. Tulips. Lips. Thick.

Breath the scent of golden corn. Sweet cum.

Spent a luxurious rainy day in bed with poet crush Joe [Brainard]. His letters. "With love, Joe."

"Is there a reason I'm in this room right now, shouldn't I be doing something?"

So programmed I look for it, completely forgetting that the day is mine… I'd spent days on end laying down reading through my childhood, teens, what I suppose was mistaken for doing nothing.

*

Not having the privilege of Joe's ballscent all over my face (she would never wash), it's a joy to hear others have.

"At any rate—I've been doing these drawings for Gay Sunshine all day, and just want to tell you what a help you've been: you down under the table all day, licking and sucking and eating me all over, below my waist. Just how I like you best in my fantasies: cleaning out my asshole, licking my feet, sucking my dick, and hungrily drinking gallons of piss. Your pretty face in my crotch all day. Outrageously 'using' you, and abusing you. So—thanks a mint kid—you do it good."

Kid. "Thanks a mint kid."

Who wouldn't want to smell of every inch their lover? To never miss a drop. Let alone be recapped with loving thanks.

"You do it good." On my tombstone.

Joe and Brad (trumpet every orifice) Jesus Fucking Kitty-Key-Rist ("Face. Face! That boy's giving face.") Gooch. Before OnlyFans, alas (good fortune, she's broke). I can't imagine two more beautiful men together.

All that and a thank you note.

Gooch's own works have been queer essentials, his biographies of Frank O'Hara and most recently, Keith Haring, along with his own memoir of NYC in the 70s/80s, *Smash Cut*, an elegy centered around his first great love, filmmaker Howard Brookner.

The marquees, neon, shadows, steps, pavement, smells, people. It's always been where I've felt most expectant, alive. Possible. She dreams these avenues, streets, pungent. Yes, I thought of living there (NYC), have been invited, encouraged by a few friends, the pull is real. But, the in and out thing worked well for me, come and play and leave and return each time special, new occasions to look forward to.

*

There are fairies at the bottom of our garden!
  You cannot think how beautiful they are;
They all stand up and sing when the Fairy
    Queen and King
  Come gently floating down upon their car.
The King is very proud and *very* handsome;
  The Queen—now can you guess who that
    could be
(She's a little girl all day, but at night she
    steals away)?
        Well—it's ME!

—Rose Fyleman,
Fairies and Chimneys

Mine has always been a cock garden. Tea roses. Construction workers. Regular guys named Joe.

What a perfect spring night. Can you smell it? Earth.

It's a Morrissey night. I know, the "politics..." Don't blow that tired old smoke up my ass.

Who do you know blameless for something? Everything? I hate it too.

Stupidity haunts.

All too human and no signs (or wishes) of being other. Human failure is what we mark, remember most. That and "the wins." Not our delicate frailties scoffed at as weakness or worse. Yes, I've lived in what is called poverty my entire life, and I'm privileged. I live. A human scale is all I'm capable of. Pretty. Ugly. May we meet in kind.

Back to reading.

In her 2024 Joanne Page Lecture, *In the Field* (Knife | Fork | Book, 2025), poet Sadiqa de Meijer posits:

"What reading elicits is, on neurological imaging, difficult to distinguish from experience itself. We read the word lilac or chai and the olfactory cortex flares. The phrase *I pulled the cloth strip through the wire fence* will spur the reader's motor cortex as if it were the movement [...] Immersive reading, that collaborative solitude, shapes our consciousness—so we do live what is written."

There's several bookcases in my bedroom, the spines of which I refer to as my "GWM of a certain age collection." Genet, Rechy, Cooper, Delany, Baldwin, Holleran, Plante, White, Williams. My eyes, if not my fingers, caress them daily, my familiars, so immediate my lived experience of each one, some whom I've met, but most only through their writings.

The well-worn pages of that "unforgettable novel of men in love," the world of Charlie and Peter in Gordon Merrick's *The Lord Won't Mind*, my umpteenth copy, being afraid someone might find it shoved in the very back behind dated encyclopedias never touched.

I didn't really need to buy another copy, but found the original Avon paperback with the cover that makes me weak. It conjures. The opening tape measure scene which allows Charlie and Peter to touch each other, appreciatively, until Peter autoejaculates (is that even a thing?! Yes!).

When I think of anything even remotely queer, or feminist, or racial, or other-ed being deliberately removed from library bookshelves, this is the reason. Reading Patricia Nell Warren's sublime 70s gay romance *The Front Runner* didn't make me gay, but made it possible. Named my existence. There *are* homosexuals, queers of all races, religions, and genders in every country of this world (and beyond). And we're cumming. Bustin' a move in living rooms, everywhere.

"So my sex date with Joe and Brad this afternoon went well, how was your day?"

Kill me now. She's never been happier.

"Who's bleeding who's bleeding!"

Cut my big toenail to the quick this morning
bloody tissues in the wastebasket

Suzanne screams through the house
me laying there frozen on my top bunk

Yesterday's score at the claw machine
Cedar Point, a jackknife I knew

she'd never allow me to keep
touching the hard lump

in my shorts pocket. My secret. Slept with
the night before pulling it out, playing

with it in the morning fascinated by how
it opened, closed, snapping shut on

my forefinger bleeding bloody murder
(who knew anyone checked the waste?)

Rushed to emerg, three or four stitches later
knife gone. I guess I proved her right

not old enough after all. Secretive-
ness comes at a young age.

Bathhouse mazes, cubicle clusters light, ignite, invite new portals, orifices, points of entry, come, go, heady mix of smoke, men, poppers, disinfectant. Metallic wallpaper patterns above the urinals at the Adonis, the stairwell at the Gaiety the hope that your boy might appear a dance and a smile between reel-to-reel filmstrips whirring at the peeps porn shot on film with stop/start title cards, grainy jump-cuts, farm boys, filthy "well worn" work jeans, boots and the studs who wear them… horny. Skinny dirtbags. Lee Ryder by mail order projected on this john's bedroom wall as he blew me and afterwards played standards on his Wurlitzer electric organ as I used the bathroom before leaving.

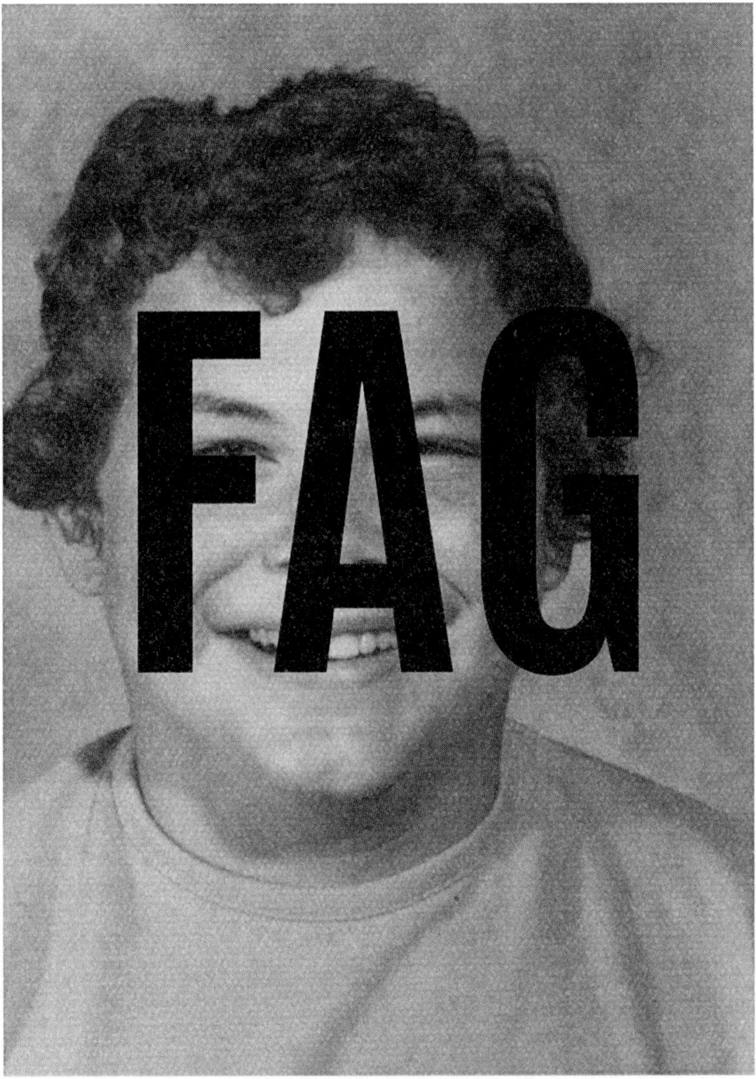
FAG

Fairy Fresh

You always think you're too much because you've always been told you're too much when in point of fact it's your being here at all that is too much for most and you know damn well you haven't come anywhere near your own idea, nay lived experience, not even close to the ceiling of what you yourself might actually consider to be too much. Who gets to fucking decide? Well. Ideally, *you* baby. You are the owner of the body where you currently reside. I don't see no "up for grabs" bin. But when you're a five-year-old in a hospital bed being the good li'l boy who smiles a lot and hears nothing but others in pain getting ALL the attention, staying quiet, while it may seem helpful for a time, for everybody else, it all becomes a li'l too much for you, you don't juggle red rubber balls on a unicycle in this circus and you don't want to be here for it. What if the pain is real? And it's yours? Mom says, "It's just a cut, it'll be alright. You'll be fine." Fairy says, "Girl, you've always been too much. Own it. Hell yes your pain is real. Welcome. Got any Sweet'n Low? Gimme more." This way >>>

Crushes

"a radical queer hustler, addict in a torn T"

"an outlaw on every front"

"magnetic and scary [...] the most extreme person I had ever encountered."

Was there ever more exquisite a creature than "the notorious" Mark Morrisroe?

*

Morrisroe: "It kills me to look at my old photographs of myself and my friends. We were such beautiful, sexy kids but we always felt bad because we thought we were ugly at the time. It was because we were such outcasts in high school and so unpopular. We believed what other people said. If any one of us could have seen how attractive we really were we might have made something better of our lives. I'm the only guy I know that wanted to run away to be a prostitute."

The dream to get out of this place, run off to the big city, an island, a life of your own making.

NYC, hustler, performance artist, photographer. Dead at 30. AIDS.

We were born the same year, 1959.

My favourite photo by Mark, a self-portrait, snapped in the back of a tub reclining on a glorious floral robe, muted plum grey-greens softly lit. Such beauty.

They wanted us silenced then, and now.

No LGBTQ+ books, programs, hotline, flags, fags.

Erase. Eradicate. Obliterate.

Sure, you can stay as long as you don't say anything. Not a word.

As if.

"We believed what other people said."

What if you were as frightened of being gay as not being straight?

You didn't fit into that world either, the majority of them simply wanted to pass to replicate heteronormativity.

Marriage. Family. Kids.

Not that there's anything wrong with that. [Insert *Three's Company* laugh track]. Being straight—not normal, but common.

Then again, how does anyone get to know who they even are, or what they really want past their upbringing?

Mostly it's "I know I'm not that!"

Such odds.

Mark, today it's exactly the same. "Sexy kids" your age all outcasts all lucky to have a dream, a night out, a good time without incident. Violence.

Mark, I carry your flame in me.

*

She almost forgot there were straight people.

Here's how insidious.

I'm watching an episode of *Drag Race*, it's the finale (All Stars 10,000) and the queens are slaying for the big bucks.

I've worked clubs, guarded the drag queens' change room, and there's nothing like hearing the conversations once a drag queen exits… SLASH SLASH SLASH! Blood splatters everywhere. Laughter. Next.

My sadness? Something in me still stops breathing at HOW GAY.

Flamers. Queens. Sissyboys. Faggots. Tenacious as fuck. Or clever. Or dead.

Every pore of my being wants the human stain of hate to be absent.

I emceed in drag at our university's summer stage cabaret *Mary Mary* (based on Bette Midler limericks), striped knitted one-piece, bowl hat with cherries, full beard and a belly laugh.

A shout from the audience, "What if your mother saw you right now?"

"She's right here in the front row! Say hello Mama!"

To find that the world's discomfort still has its root cellar in me.

"Why do you have to be so gay all the time?" Like it's something to moderate, turn off at will.

Fags. Waterboarded any given moment of every single day.

Girl, not even masked ICE agents could make me less homosexual.

What she is is a cocksuckin' fag on Uniform Night. Line up.

Diane Keaton lost her Oscar for *Looking For Mr. Goodbar*. Like Rex Reed, they knew then, "There is no god."

There must be gay ICE agents. (Now, that thought makes me shudder, the hatred that must reside there. Mercy.)

We were supposed to be cured.

Love me some cured meats.

Here's what we now know. With certainty. We do not learn from history. It only tells us stories. On repeat (not shuffle).

Has the world changed?

Only ever in climates. All, repeatedly wiped out, in
an instant. One falls, another tide rises.

*

It's a Sunday afternoon in July. Off my balcony,

"men" dress in their best boy gear:

ball cap cut-offs, ringed socks in boots

head for the bbq at The Eagle usually

jovial crowd, a Purdy's gay assortment,

your daddies, twinks, bears, otters, puppies,

leather queens/dudes, regs and visitors.

There once was a wading pool till "boys will be boys"

shoved each other in as they passed, bursting

its sides flooding the dance floor below.

I have such an affinity for blokes out

for a good time (one hopes) camaraderie a break

from it all each their own stories that brought

them out (very few born here) “family day”

the hour shifts, retro night spins

classics you danced/fucked to on poppers

at the Barn, Rock ‘n Roll Fag Bar, Zippers,

Komrads, Club Colby’s, Joy, Cornelius, Stages,

The Manatee, The Toolbox, The Quest,

The Club Baths, The Romans, Spa on Maitland,

Boots, Chaps, tea dances, nights and nights

may this night never end.

*

Dawn.

There’s this 2025 documentary on how US queers feel about the American Flag.

It's well meaning, with moments that ring true.

She can still well up over the promise of America.

She's read. Not dead.

Like pretty much every war, the Civil War never ended.

Americans only know how to do one thing.

Struggle.

They fight over/for everything. Even their rights.

Why o why would anyone have to fight just to be. Here.

Every oppressed people I know of, us "underlings."

Those who simply seek to enjoy their everyday lives without harm or fear. Food at their table. A place to rest their head.

You know. Home.

I never dreamed of power over. Even in my raunchiest fantasies exercising breath control when there's nothing but his cock ruling my windpipe, where I know he'll respect my tap out, show mercy, pause before he takes me again.

The rules/laws are clear. Trust, baby. We both get what we want. Fuck. Bliss out. Cocksucker tears.

Those fuckers slashed the suicide hotlines for vets, LGBTQ+ people.

That's what they choose to do with their power.

Frociaggine

For a hot minute
she forgot there
were such cross
loathsome "I don't
know these people"
bibles out to burst
queer bubbles
all so tragically familiar
at my tender age
yet is it really so
strange to think you
have a right to sit
in the light of day
without violence?

I Want To Be A Faggot When I Grow Up

Make no mistake, it was the church that made me into the homosexual I am.

O, she was already a Mo… from my premie birth on the toilet baptized (all three times) a true homosexual.

The church just taught me the good stuff. Majesty. Grandeur. Idolatry. The pipe organ. Set design!

All that AND the Sweet Baby Jesus!

*

I overheard her say,

"Did you hear about the guy who killed himself for being a homosexual?"

I point my revolver, fire five slugs into the fundamentalist's head,

disfigure the believer unrecognizable except for the fingerprints on

her blood-drenched bible.

Did you hear about the faggot who shot the fundamentalist to death

in honour of his lover who hung himself because he had no home?

Adam's Feet

A church pew. A dining table. Lilies in a glass vase.

"Did you say fifty?"

Five zero? plus elegant torsos   names that end
in a vowel   with a Z   gunned down
single shooter?   gay club

"I won't miss fucking Florida."
How can I write about
                                        anything?

Adam's feet are beside me   within reach.
I touched one today   a greeting
He's married   a daughter

Fags have been shot for less

If he had a gun he could killmenow
tell the cops I came on to him
leave here   kill a few more   fifty more.

The shooter so disgusted
at the sight of two men kissing
"In front of his family"

His father told the press
enough to annihilate fifty.
All fifty states Lt. Gov. Texas tweets

"They shall reap what they sow."
Trump congratulates himself   blames Obama
taking America down this bridal path

Adam
it is so much fun to have a crush on you
(Don't you love crushes?)

I will take that photo of you to really look at your
olive skin   your neck and feet without fear
of being

mowed down   shot to death   slain this dismal
blissful place   genderqueers pay some
straight hole in the wall   dance

their tits off   neck   DON'T THINK
of the ugliness that borders   infringes
every six-year-old in a classroom

every Black male pulled over   every female
in uniform   every campus   workplace   street corner
storefront   bible study   home

Fifty rounds a minute/cut down in as many seconds
Like you I have been a moving target my whole life
at OCAD gunsights drawn on my face   my back

I left America.
I knew I had no future
that Americans mean it when they say

'Love it or leave it'

That Nancy's Ronnie and his kind wilfully
turned   left us to die   and I will.
A nancy boy. A faggot.

One. Glorious. Flame.

Cockaholic

This is my first meeting—it's difficult and all, so bear with me. Breathe. Okay.

Hello. My name is Jeff K. And I'm a cockaholic.

I admit that I am absolutely powerless in the face of dick.

I can't help myself. I see a guy's bulge and everything comes to a complete stop. I lose it. All control.

In awe, the world disappears leaving this hard fierce radiant object, drops me to a crawl, lips reach—suddenly I remember the first time I wanted something, anything with my mouth: daddy's finger, my own fist, a blue rubber ring, Jesus, anything, just stick it in front of me.

There must've been some pivotal moment when not just anything could appease my taste buds. I only knew my mouth wanted cock. No substitutes.

It helps that I'm gay.

I don't know why, didn't care really, but everybody around me wanted to know why, except for the thousands of married men I sucked off. They didn't care either.

"Boy, if my wife could do this."

Look, you're not proving anything by having a wife or girlfriend. I mean, I believe you're straight, I can taste Brut, but don't compliment me by comparing me to your spouse. Of course I'm going to suck your dick better. I *want* to suck it! I'm not legally obligated to servitude. Next.

After meeting hundreds of thousands of dicks, you'd think I'd have grown tired, despondent, "you've seen one you've seen them all," right?

Whoever said that must not have been looking.

Millions of dicks, never one the same. Not even on twins. True snowflakes.

Each guy wears theirs differently. "What have we here? HELLO!"

It still seizes and moves me, the mystery of arousal. To see a meaty piece rise to the occasion.

I know it's just filling with blood, but I continue to marvel.

So, when does the circle jerk start?

Recovery? Recovery from what?

What's that?… can I go a day with out dick? Why would anyone want to?

Wait a sec, you want me to abstain from cock for how long? Three months? I'm not vegetarian, Cher. You trying to kill me? And no jacking off? Get real, I'm here because I thought you guys liked dick.

You love cock, but you're trying not to have any. Okay, give it to me!

"There's more to life than sex." Ain't that a kicker.

I fucking hate that, like it's some profound truth everyone subscribes to in blind faith, the final word that stops talk show hosts dead mid-sentence.

There's absolutely no data to substantiate that there must be more to life.

None.

In fact, I'm willing to bet that all enjoyment that really matters comes from unceasing, limitless creative acts of sexual delight, and that everything else is intermission.

Sure, there's work, but why do you think they invented work? To keep people from pleasuring themselves all the livelong day. Now we just have sex in the workplace and they're trying to criminalize that.

"It shouldn't rule your life."

I can think of worse rulers.

Reagan. Mulroney. Hell, the Pope goes around pretending he doesn't have a dick. Look how fucked-up Catholics are.

If you guys are religious, why don't you simply worship what you say you love. My dick could use a little.

Hey! What happened to that crosstalk rule, it's my turn to speak.

You want me to leave?

What, you scared of a little dick? Me, too!

Okay, I'm outta here. Come find me afterwards, we'll shake some bushes in the park.

BONEGUPPY

Gigs

My first gig in Toronto was a solo show at The Rivoli. *GWM* was performed naked in a bathtub, followed by *Anal Pleasures* at the Cabana Room on Spadina. Soon after I premiered *The Battle of the Flesh* at The Music Gallery, had a few stints at Rhubarb!, launched *Cock & Soul* at This Ain't the Rosedale Library, sat in bath towels at the Spa on Maitland passing poppers for *The World is Fucked and Sometimes Beautiful.* The poets may remember *She's Having A Doris Day* in Kensington Market with CAConrad, my "buddy-booth" sex tour on the streets of Montreal (*This Is Where I Get Off*), the go-go boys at KFB, or launching *Poetry Is Queer* with a ukulele band in Harbourville, Nova Scotia. I'm now thrilled to announce the Official Toronto Launch of *PIQ* at my local haunt on the street where I live, The Black Eagle. Don Pyle will serving music, and yes, I'll be serving up Kirby. All are welcome.

Simple Enough

was first performed on December 7, 1985 at the Collingwood Arts Centre, Toledo, Ohio. Performed by Jeffrey J. Albright, directed by the author. Kirby premiered this in Canada on July 30, 1986 at The Rivoli, Toronto, in an evening called GWM. *Staging by Reid Diamond. Masks by Rebecca Diederichs.*

I'm twenty-one years old.
A man in an army jacket plays
with my nipples, wants to take me home,
tie me up and fuck my ass. Says
he'll be nice to me. Part of me
is scared, a bigger part wants
to be humiliated, a blind willing mouth
to his Russian roulette. I live to worship
a good servant. Then I notice small cuts
along his wrists marked with dry blood.
I choke and want to throw up.
My nipples are still bruised.

*

I'm nineteen. We play twenty questions.
Girl asks what's it like for me to be
with a man. She's Catholic. I'm the only fag.

As long as I joke about it, it's cool
with everyone else. I love the strength
when a man holds me, the angularity
of his features, the energy
of male passion, the immediacy of sex.
The play of two powers that submit
and penetrate… nobody's laughing.

*

I'm seventeen, in love with a boy
who wants to be a minister.
I'd make a good pastor's wife.
I think he likes me. Drunk, he lets
me put my head on his shoulder.
"You remind me of my old girlfriend."
He tells me he's not gay. I don't want
him to be. I just want to love him.

*

I'm fifteen. It's dark.
I'm in the arcade of an adult
peep show. For each quarter
I drop, nameless people fuck
for fifty seconds on a cum-stained
screen. I'm here cause the men
here want their cocks sucked,
one of many stops to find

others looking for the same.
Besides, I don't know where else
to find men who are like me.

This boy in the film has a big one
and a smile to go with
which really turns me on.
A man stands outside my booth,
a flimsy half-curtain between us.
He wants me, but he's older
and much bigger than me. Maybe
he has a knife. Maybe he wants
to kill me. The film stops.
I close my eyes, pull the curtain aside.

The man is Jesus. He embraces
me, tells me I'm his own.

*

I'm twelve years old. Each year I tell
myself this is the summer I'm going
to suck cock. I'm the pudgy kid
who stands by the fence at the Rec
Centre pool, spends the entire day
stealing glances at my favourite boy
lifeguard. I want him so bad. At night,
wet dreams bury my face sniffing

the nylon pouch between his legs.
I hate myself for letting
another summer pass. And fall.

*

I'm nine. My secret place is a tent
tied to the rafters up in the attic.
Inside I read Secret Sea
by Robb White. I want to be a sailor.
I read and read and read. I love
reading. Outside the light of my tent
it's become night. I'm afraid
of the dark. No one else knows this
but Paul McCartney is dead in my attic.
He only comes out at night. He waits
for me. Mom calls up for me to come
down. I cannot leave the tent.
I don't want him to know that I know.

*

I'm seven. I play by myself down
In the basement. There's a small
room with pink paint I flake
off damp concrete walls.
There's a rusty sink and shower
that "we don't use." I take off all my

clothes and pretend I'm forced
to stand under just the hot water.
And then just the cold water to see
how much I can take. I am a very strong boy.

*

I'm five. I love my kindergarten teacher
Mrs. MacGregor. She calls me
"Little Sunshine." I go to the hospital
to get my tonsils out. I'm thin
and very sick. For one month I get
to eat mashed potatoes with butter.
I love them. First day back I race
into the classroom. Mrs. MacGregor
asks who I am. She doesn't remember
me. I'm her little sunshine.

*

I am two, in a large room
with other sick children. My mother sits
on my bed beside me, feeds me tuna
salad on soft white bread. I live to be
with her.
                    I wake to a dark room.
It is night. My mother is gone.
Harsh light pierces a door ajar
at the other end of the room.

I hear voices. I hear my mother.
I call out to her. The door closes.
I lie there in the dark. Alone.

*

I'm twenty-six years old.
The most beautiful man in the world
loves me. He thinks I'm gorgeous.
I love him and want to believe him.
I've always wanted to share
my life with someone.

The Battle of the Flesh

was first performed by the author July 31, 1987, at The Music Gallery, Toronto. Directed by Peter Jenkins.

PLACE: A toilet stall in a men's public washroom (with gloryhole).

TIME: 1987

Last night at the urinals this guy pulls out, shoots his load away from my face. "AIDS, you know."

No, I don't know what it's like to be told you're dead. To think the next cumshot may be fatal. To see this boy's hot inviting cock—a loaded special aimed to kill.

No. I don't know what lesions may appear in the morning.

[Sound: gunshot].

It happened one morning, me racing through the house wailing, screaming bloody murder, tears streaming across my cheeks. My father had to tackle me, hold me down just long enough to get my penis uncaught from my zipper.

Fear. Not fear of AIDS. I don't give myself reason to fear. My fear is their fear of me and how far they will go to rid themselves of this fear.

Who are *they*?

They are the creators of this poster. [SLIDE 1: Metro AIDS poster depicting a young heterosexual couple]. Nice, huh? Big. Glossy. Now, given these three choices, can you pick the missing object from this poster? A) An elephant B) A duck C) A fag. Certainly there are homosexual Daffys and Dumbos, but C here is the correct answer. I am missing from this poster. I, a homosexual male who represents over 90% of all known cases of AIDS across Canada, don't exist in ANY of Metro's display advertising concerning the public prevention of AIDS. In their perfect world, I don't exist. I am undesirable. I am expendable. To them, I brought this disease upon myself. To them, I deserve to die. [Actor refers to male model in slide]. Fuck is he cute! [Actor steps into project slide image opposite male]. Don't we make a lovely couple?

I'm responsible for AIDS. Yep, me personally. After fucking a green monkey while vacationing in the Congo, I spent a luxurious week in the Big Apple being pissed and shit on in the backroom bathtub of the Mineshaft with an inhaler of butyl nitrate taped to my left nostril, eating three square meals (based on USDA government regulations) of pork with applesauce from a rusty tin, while a seventeen year old corn-fed unemployed farm boy from Ohio fucked my ass without a condom, stuffing the dead gerbil that suffocated there two days earlier further up my bum as a Vietnam vet shared the needle he found on the floor to shoot smack up my left arm. Then I came home and fucked your boyfriend who in turn was sucked off by a Baptist minister (to cover his tuition) who then left his wife and children to run off with the ninth grade Sunday School instructor who still turns tricks on the side.

That green monkey. Must have been gay.

It's not me I fear for. I'm well. But inside me, a fourteen-year-old cries "Don't touch me. I don't want to be gay. I don't want to die." I am still gay. The disease doesn't change that. There are gay people like myself who continue to live. Who continue to count the losses.

We have seen the face of AIDS. It is the face of our lovers.

I'm at St. Michael's. John asks me to stop on the way and pick up three chilli dogs for a buck and a quarter at the 7-11. He has Kaposi's. A visitor seated across from me has Kaposi's. I'm well. "Why do you think this thing is running so rampant among gay men," John asks. "What, this craving for chilli dogs?" We talk about the kinkiest things we've ever done. John admits to being fisted, which shocks the shit out of me. I mean, here's this boy, 5'8" max and with his frame? You'd think anyone's fist would split him in two. A visitor, Barry, wittily describes himself as a "park analyst." It didn't take long for me to conjure images of his hairy bum being lovingly offered over various altars of dead tree limbs, tulip beds. Me, I'm the novice of our troupe. My idea of kink is sucking off some jock in the showers as the team lines up for training, but this doesn't answer John's question: what happened that allowed scores of gay men to succumb to AIDS? Is it something I've done? Do my locker room fantasies cause people harm? Am I the pervert they say I am?

You see, they think all this is because I put my peepee in your mouth and you put yours up my bum. These are the very same people who believe that because you and I play with each other, not only are we going to die, we're going to burn in hell. They believe that as long as they keep it contained among the "undesirables"—the fags, the blacks, the junkies, and whores—AIDS may just be the answer to their "social problem." Someone along the way told them I was a bad person, and they have told others I'm bad. And for a long time, I believed them.

At University Pub last night. A group called the "Wet Shavers." Predominantly straight college crowd.

Girls in big Belinda Carlisle sweaters dance while guys drink on the sidelines, pick potential fucks. On my way out the door, some beastie boy grabs me by the shirt and yells in my face, "DO YOU HAVE AIDS FAG?", his laugh reeking of stale draught.

He doesn't know I could kill him.

Yeah you, you breeder fuck. You think you're a man because you pump pussy like it was a god-given right, like you own it. And you fuck and marry and fuck someone else and get divorced and marry again and somewhere along the line the babies get baptized and you vow to raise them like good Christians, but that was two wives and countless fucks ago (not to mention the kids that didn't make it) and why not? It's all perfectly legal, perfectly acceptable heterosexual behaviour, protected by the letter of the law and sanctioned by the Church. And maybe you have a brother-in-law who's "one of those" and you think he's okay just as long as he doesn't talk about it, as long as he doesn't bring his faggot friend to family gatherings. You're so much better than me you make me sick to my stomach. Go ahead, tell your kids you love them as you file for divorce. I mean your world is so fucking perfect I want to cheer the next wedding party that honks its horns and flaunts it in my face. You tell your AIDS jokes just loud enough so I can overhear and you're so fucking outrageously funny you make me want to die. Did you hear that? You make me want to die.

But I'm not going to die of AIDS.

You can't make me.

Someone along the way told me they were better than me. I no longer believe them.

Here's something you can try this at home. All you need is one or two pillows and any medium-size sports racket of your choice. I prefer a tennis racket because of its length. Just place the pillow in front of you and hold the racket in both hands, like so. Don't think about this, just do it. Thinking keeps you from acting. See, I'm thinking about it and nothing's happening. Don't think.

[Strike pillow with racket repeatedly].

THEY LIE, WE DIE!

[Repeat until exhausted].

[Actor writes THEY LIE, WE DIE on toilet stall partition].

There. Now we can move on.

The perversity is the heterosexual belief that human life is expendable.

The perversity is medical doctors who refuse emergency surgery because they suspect their patient might be queer, even after testing negative for AIDS.

The perversity is that *to this day* my healthy blood is considered contaminated by the Red Cross because I'm labelled "high risk."

The perversity is that most assume I already carry the virus or I'm at risk of getting the virus or I'm passing on the virus, that I'm gay and therefore guilty.

There is perverseness in lies.

THEY LIE, WE DIE. NO! THEY LIE. I'm not going to die of AIDS.

I know you're thinking "But I've been with fifteen-zillion men in the past five years, two of which suggested a condom but already came." This means you're already a victim. Not of AIDS. But of fear. AIDS breeds fear. It loves fear.

I dated this guy, Peter. Cute boy. Young. Blonde. Nice dick. We met through this hole (a gloryhole through a toilet stall partition). He was constantly afraid of getting AIDS, had been with someone who'd already died of complications of the disease and in Peter's mind his own diagnosis was inevitable. I ran into him a few months ago, "Hi!"–"Hi." I knew something was wrong. A mutual friend tells me Peter's wigging out over some pre-AIDS condition, some swelling, but Peter's convinced he's already as good as dead, and has maxed out all his cards, told his friends to fuck off, that he's returning to Australia to end it all.

I don't fault Peter, not one bit. The constant demand and pressure of being other, homosexual, morally wrong, high risk, sinner, sick, has armed a culture that can't say gay and not think AIDS in the same breath. What chances do Peter, do any of us, have?

I know what you're thinking. I know what you're thinking betcha he's a carrier, betcha he's a carrier... I bet you he has it. I mean chances are he's fooled around with guys who think they have it. Aren't you afraid you have it? Fear. Licking us up one side and down the other.

Am I fucking you? Then it's none of your fucking business.

Fucking. Fucking sorry story.

First, the good news. What we have for you is Mr. Safe. [Show condom]. Mr. Safe is here to protect us from Mr. Virus. Here's how it works. [Knocks on toilet partition, ginormous stuffed cock comes through glory hole]. It's Mr. Big! Hello Mr. Big, I'd like to introduce you to Mr. Safe. I sure hope you two are compatible! [Struggles to slip condom over stuffed cock that gets bigger and bigger]. OMG, it's the MYTHICAL MONSTER COCK! I've been looking and looking and looking… TELL ME YOU'RE NEGATIVE! Wait. Get a grip. Check your Safe Sex Manual: Monster Cock, page 42, "If condom is too small, kneel and pant." [Pants]. Are you close? [Pants more]. You get the feeling there's something left wanting? [Checks manual]. "If he comes, duck and cover." [Ducks]. Is it safe?

Yes, condoms are essential. They provide an answer to an immediate need: protection.

But, just what am I protecting? Myself, and the guy I'm with. But why is that necessary?

Well, maybe I'm worth protecting, and his life is worth protecting too. I love who I am and honour the life of the man I share myself with, even if it's only for a brief moment. Share my honour. There's no question of risk.

[SLIDES 2,3,4 showing actor as child]. I'm running

through the ruins of a bombed out shelter in search of an oracle to deliver us from this plague. [A thin voice calls out from the rubble. I start digging, pulling away at rocks. A child's face stares at me through iron mesh. I reach through. She pulls away]. Because this one child with AIDS has been shunned by the world, the world continues to perish.

Who will answer for this child?

WHO WILL ANSWER FOR THIS CHILD?

"Dad, when I grow up can I be gay like you and Donald?"

"You can be anything you want to be, Tommy."

"Can I be a girl?"

"You can be anything you want to be."

"I want to be gay just like you," they smile, feel the stubble on my cheek.

And I think to myself, don't be afraid, this is your child.

"That's good, Tommy."

Body Positive

was first performed by the author on February 24, 1988, at The Rhubarb! Festival, Buddies in Bad Times Theatre, Toronto.

I can tell you exactly how I got it. From my mother. Each week she sent me dozens of clippings from the various rags she read and swore by: "NO CURE FOR GAYS IN SIGHT," "Rescuers to Wear Anti-AIDS Gloves," "Homosexuals Converted By AIDS Scare…"

"But Mom, I don't have AIDS."

"You had no trouble telling me you're a gay, now why can't you tell me you have AIDS?"

My diagnosis came several months ago. I already knew, because I'd been through all of this with Mark. Same signs. Symptoms. Called in sick so often that I lost my job. I've been down here ever since.

The vigil. It began two years ago. Two PWAs chained themselves to the doors of the Old Federal Building in protest towards the government's total lack of response to its "number one health priority." Dozens of us have chained ourselves since. Twenty-one have died. Most of us have been arrested. Security guards in rubber gloves come with a pair of bolt cutters around noon each day. They think the gloves will protect them.

[Through bullhorn] "Arresting us is not going to get rid of us!"

My friend Eric was arrested last Friday. They came out with the cutters, snipped the chains, took him inside and booked him. The fine, twenty-five dollars.

"What are they going to do? Kill me if I don't pay it?"

My first arrest, I plead not guilty. I *am* not guilty. The people who work in this building are guilty. The pharmaceutical companies are guilty. Their bosses are guilty.

[Bullhorn] "If anyone should be fined it's the fucking President of the United States. The man who would be king!"

There. That'll bring out the cutters.

I'm here because I want them to have to see me, to look my life in the fucking face. I'm not going to go until I'm ready. Until I'm heard.

Mark and I met at a Sunday afternoon tea dance, like a scene out of *West Side Story*. From across a crowded floor. He stood against the window facing

Polk Street with short-cropped sandy-brown hair and a white t-shirt and cut-offs. Me? I was on the floor doing the courtship dance of my life! Mark smiled, joined me, "I love the way you move."

At his place I lay on his futon. He stepped out wearing these amazingly thick broad-rimmed glasses and at first I want to seriously laugh, but then I thought, wow, this is really cool, I mean he doesn't even know me and he can strut in these silly glasses and not even think about it.

Then and there, I knew I could do his laundry.

Mark's diagnosis came in late April. A flu that wouldn't go away. Increasing fatigue and diarrhea in May, hospitalization in June, pneumocystis, dehydration, inability to absorb nutrients. The Kaposi's led to chemo in July and August.

The night before his first treatment, Mark asked me to wash his hair. It became our Friday night ritual. He loved the feel of my hands caressing his scalp. Tenderly. It was the most intimate thing we could do at the time.

Home became a series of reprieves for Mark, but his weight, his strength ebbed (HOW DO WE STOP THIS GODDAMN DIARRHEA! GOD IT'S SO

PAINFUL…"). Once he called me into his room, and just sat there glaring at his reflection in the mirror. "I always wanted to see my cheekbones before I died." Mark doing his best Joan Crawford. We pissed ourselves laughing, I mean we really did!

Then during his second bout of pneumonia Mark took his own life. What little he had left. He wanted to live life on his terms, and told me that when the lesions reached his face, he was done. "I'm too vain, you understand, yes?" "Yes, yes, I understand."

You know Mark, I don't think anyone understands. I don't think anyone allows themself to understand.

When I was a small child, my mom always told me, "Sometimes the truth hurts. But you always have to tell the truth, even if it hurts."

And people, friends, come up to me, tell me how courageous I am. At Mark's memorial, friends (for whom Mark's was only one out of four services they attended that week) expressed their remote sympathy, asked me if I was "okay," my whole body screaming "Okay?! No, I'm not okay."

That is, until this one woman, Jill, who knew Mark, worked with him, looked me in the face and said, "This really sucks."

Yeah, she's right. This really *does* suck.

I sit here, chained, my body pleading for new drugs that will feed it some hope as people push Bibles in my face. They don't give a flying fuck if I die or not. To them, I'm just a degenerate fag who likes to take it up the ass "like a woman."

Well, I'm alive goddammit. I'm alive! I'm a person living with AIDS and I'm alive! I'm a gay man with AIDS and look what I can do. I can chain myself to the front doors of the Old Federal Building and scream!

[Bullhorn] "YOU FEEL SO SAFE IN YOUR LEATHER-CUSHIONED SEATS YOU POMPOUS IGNORANTS FUCKS, LOOK AT ME! I AM THE GENERAL PUBLIC YOU USELESS ASSHOLES AND I'M ALIVE! YOUR SILENCE HASN'T KILLED ME YET!"

[Reads from news clipping] "Scott W. left us recently after a nine month battle with AIDS. Scott took an active part in the ongoing AIDS vigil at the Old Federal Building downtown. He will always be remembered by his chosen family and friends for his outspoken, generous spirit, good humour, and concern for others. A memorial gathering for Scott will be held at the Lesbian and Gay Community Center on Monday, March 1 at 2pm."

I don't want you to die.

I won't have it.

Bob Smith Sucks Cock

was first performed by the author on February 15, 1989 at The Rhubarb! Festival, Buddies in Bad Times Theatre, Toronto.

"Do you want it? Do you wanna suck on it? Go ahead, Bobby. I won't tell anyone. Promise. C'mon Bobby, I thought we were buddies. Put it in your mouth. You know you want to. No, I'm not going to piss! Okay, okay Bobby… I guess you don't want to be in the club. Just lick it for me then, just a little bit. I won't force you, look, where are my hands? You can kill me if I say anything Bobby cuz I ain't going to tell anyone!"

[Lights up on graffiti: Bob Smith SUCKS COCK]

I knew I always wanted to suck cock… and I guess I knew I'd be good at it.

"I'm tellin' you he's a fag. He sucked Johnny's dick. He's a cocksuckin' fag. I always knew he was queer…"

You told me you wouldn't tell anyone.

"Have you seen him? The cocksucker? If that fuckin'

fag comes anywheres fuckin' near me I'll bash his fuckin' head in!"

I didn't do it. I didn't! I sure wanted to. It was right there sticking out of the fly in his jeans. Christ he was beautiful.

"Go ahead Bobby, take it in your mouth."

Right there. I still kick myself for not doing it. That perfect moment. I thought I must've been imagining things and it was at that exact moment when my lips first reached to meet flesh… they parted, went from dry to moist… magically began to make those little motions they were born to make.

Make me! I bet you can't make me do it!

"You faggot. You want to do it. Wait 'til everyone in school finds out you're a fag."

I think Johnny was as scared as me.

That night I knelt beside my bed, licked the pool of cum I'd shot in my hand. Johnny you taste so good…

I want to please you / to press your socked feet in my face and sniff / pre-come smear your fingers /

tug that tiny trail of hair at your navel / lick the arch of your ribcage / nuzzle your armpit / tongue your bicep / buttocks clench / lift your pelvis / an offering? / (you know exactly what I want) / my eyes beg to please / to adore / to soak your sex straining through white cotton / sucking on two, three fingers / locked by your eyes / always checking for some sign to please / a smile, a caress.

An order / your hand presses my face to your crotch / rubbing your cock knowing / knowing what it means / for me to be possessed / to be yours / to be for you / please, please let me / do you know how beautiful you are / how beautiful your cock is / how much you please me / please please.

No. Not yet.

I just want to see you stroke yourself / to make me wet for you / to make my lips beg / to touch it to my lips wet / wet.

Do you want it? Do you want to be my cocksucker? Take it, yeah, suck my cock, yeah god you feel so good (yeah god…).

Do you know what you do to me? Do you know how much it means for you to offer your sex your manhood your power over me through me taking me demanding I swallow more more to take it all and plead for more please please.

Don't come yet. Let me see it hold it firm slap my face bury my nostrils balls sopping wet wanting so much to eat your ass have you squirt all over my face my chest my mouth put it in my mouth to gently suck.

Let me sleep with your sex in my face keep it safe warm safe moist safe.

Hold my head and let me feel you breathe.

Am I good? Am I a good cocksucker? My mouth was made to be filled by you owned by you please please did I please you? Is it okay? Was it any good? Can I be your cocksucker? Yours? Please? Everyday, I want to please you every single day. I'll do anything to please you I'll try harder, let me try, please, please.

Fuck.

For years I've been trying to please 'til my face was fucked numb. Wanting to please you, and you, and the whole fucking world.

I tricked with this guy named Bill.

I guess he sensed I was a little nervous and I was because I'd never had sex in a bed before, only hook-ups in parks, washrooms, stairwells. I was just being a cocksucker.

I think Bill wanted me to fuck him, my first clue being his ankles on my shoulders, but I didn't have any confidence being a top. I'd just never fucked anyone before, not on my menu, and I'm limp. "You okay?" I said I didn't think I could do what he wanted. He laughed, "Hey silly, I want to please you too. We're making love Bob. Enjoy it."

My mind went blank. You mean it doesn't matter whether I fuck him or he fucks me or if I stay hard or if he comes? You mean I don't have to try to please?

[To dick] Did you hear that?

I'm Bob Smith. I'm a cocksucker. A damn fine cocksucker. Now, I want all of you to know this, because maybe you can't tell just by looking at me and I don't want you to miss your chance. I mean, I'm really good. I even provide a guarantee. Yessireebob! If I'm not the absolute best blowjob you've ever had, I'll do it again until I get it down. I'll work to your exact specifications and mine.

It will be my pleasure.

Wait a sec… (checking out guy in audience). Don't I know you? Sure, second floor men's room, U of M, Ann Arbor… not very long but thick, a strong ridge carrying the shaft.

He said he couldn't come. I told him that was okay.

Spew

was first performed by the author on July 22, 1992 at Buddies in Bad Times Theatre, Toronto. Directed by Damon D'Oliveira.

[Actor crouches on stage beside a pail. We hear a hum grow louder then *snap*, he vomits into the pail, retching sporadically throughout the entire monologue.]

Who says I can walk away from this? I can't fucking walk away. Do you think for one fucking minute it still matters whether I test positive or negative? Why would you bring it up then? The test! Did I pass the fucking test? I'm way past a fucking test. And how do I pass? BY testing fucking negative?! What? Is that supposed to relieve me? Will I feel fucking good about that? Something to phone home about: "Hey Mom, don't worry, it hasn't gotten me yet, no really, I'm telling you the truth. I guess I'm safe, not like those other guys… they must've done something wrong. Yeah, they should've known better, should have stopped their fucking around. I can't believe people still do that. I mean, be promiscuous." WHO THE FUCK DO YOU THINK YOU ARE? You think you're fucking better?! What the fuck do you know about it? You think you fucking know! You don't fucking know me at all. You talk to your friends as if you do. Make it all about you. Then you walk. You can walk away from it. I can't. It's in my blood. Not because I fucking tested. You still don't get it, do you? WE'RE ALL HIV+. Every one of us. Do you think after twelve years with this disease I can differentiate between affected and infected? I've been a person living with AIDS since the onset. I don't need a fucking test. I don't want one. What? You think I'm scared? No. I'm devastated. There's not another candle I can light. Not another memorial I can attend. Not another loss I'm able to stomach. I don't want them dead. I don't want any of us dead. I want them in my arms. I want their cocks spewing in my face. Their rectums pushing against my tongue. I want every orifice in my body filled. Not "just sex." Not "only sex." Not sex "to die for." WHO THE FUCK CAME UP WITH THAT LANGUAGE?! "Is that all that matters to you?" "Is that all you still think about?" "She's stuck in the seventies." "I think AIDS is the best thing that's happened to our community, I mean look at the organizations, the volunteers. Now we're learning values, how to love and care for each other." FUCKING CHRIST ARE YOU FUCKING KIDDING ME?! I CAN'T BELIEVE I'M FUCKING HEARING THIS! I MEAN I REALLY DID HEAR THIS. Kirby, it's okay, he didn't mean it, he doesn't know, he probably heard someone else say it and he's simply repeating it. People don't mean what they say, especially when they don't have anything to say. They just talk. To fill in the blank. To make up for not having anything to say. For not knowing the answer. JUST DON'T SAY ANYTHING THEN! I DON'T NEED TO HEAR YOU FUCKING TALK. YOU'RE WAY OUT OF NOT KNOWING. I DON'T NEED YOUR FUCKING WORDS. PLEASE DON'T TRY AND MAKE IT UP. DON'T TRY TO COME UP WITH AN ANSWER. A REASON. Just sit here with me. Hold my hand while I take a shit. Pray it comes. Pray it's solid. Don't you dare try and take away my anger. You can't do anything for me. I don't want you to. But if you choose to stay, then live. Not because you might die. But because you're alive. Take my cock in your hand. Look into my eyes. Breathe with me. Feel my life. Don't be afraid. I won't hurt you. Let me hold your face in my hands. Fuck, you are beautiful. Let me kiss those lesions. I'm not afraid of you. I'm not afraid. It's okay. Nothing else matters. This is it. This is all that matters. I'm here.

fight the good fight

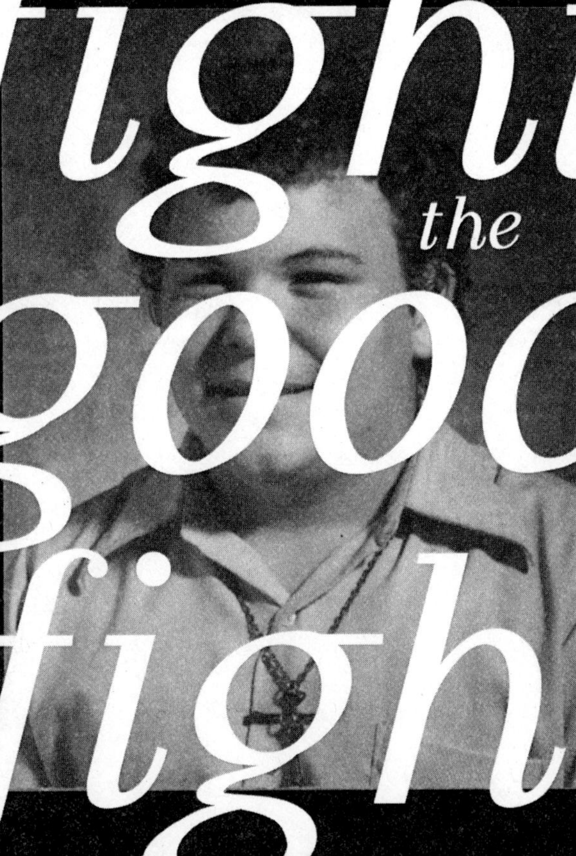

Fairy

Honestly, I just can't believe that I'm here.

So, when I enter a room…

"Surprise! Surprise! Surprise!"

(*SQUEE!* Flip-flop dance!)

"Hop in the carriage girl, we've a got a ball to attend!"

Toledo, Ohio. 1965. Their earliest Fairy inklings (in living colour on CBS), every ounce/inch of me off to meet/dance on clouds with the prince!

Rodgers & Hammerstein's *Cinderella* was my first experience of "the theatre..." the constantly moving sets and staging for TV were so peculiar, strange, unreal... and otherly glorious.

What is this place?

"Well, of course, it's Fairyland, silly! Where have you been? We've been expecting you!"

*

Toledo, Ohio. 1985. Zenobia Shriners Hall on Madison Avenue.

My youngest sister's wedding. A grand affair... a feast. It wouldn't be a reception without kielbasa from Smitty's, open bar, live music, cake, and the chicken dance. Couple of hundred in attendance, mostly family and friends, buddies of the groom from West Point, business associates.

And there I am, in the wedding party, seated at the front table decked out in a tux looking like a million bucks, the only one 'uncoupled' by law, though it would be more accurate to say in a (gay) partnership that's unrecognized, not celebrated in any way as open as tonight's occasion.

No biggie. Nothing special, personal. Just a declaration of love and commitment celebrated by most if not all this festive night. The very thing many plan their whole lives around.

Some, repeatedly so.

The heaviness of this kind of slight increases incrementally each successive year, each and every family holiday outing. On Christmas Eve I'll check my watch for the "respectable" hour to leave, head towards a gay bar, rejoice with "my kind."

But this is in no way about me. I'm here to celebrate my sister's happiness, her high school sweetheart, my family, my hometown.

Then, it's the bride and groom's first dance.

I can't honestly recall the number... could've been that Peabo Bryson & Roberta Flack 80s wedding classic:

Tonight, I celebrate my love for you
It seems the natural thing to do
Tonight, no one's gonna find us
We'll leave the world behind us
When I make love to you

Only now reading the lyrics… it's practically a gay torch song!

Then I feel someone come up behind me, move the chair from the table, escort me onto the dance floor.

My love. My leading man. The man who takes me in his arms, holds me, fills my heart, guides my feet in a slow dance.

Don Pyle. There is no one braver.

So much braver than myself. I would have never.

But you, my love, knew that to celebrate, we had to dance. Didn't give it a second thought.

I overheard a cousin say, "This is so unfair to [my sister]." That we were somehow dancing to make a statement.

What statement might that be?

Did they think for one second I was going to deny my partner (myself?) this magic moment? His invitation to dance? My own sister's wedding?

"Where's the conga line?!"

No, it wasn't planned. We never discussed it.

Scared shitless, eyes closed the entire time, I was thankful Don was that much taller… how my face could nuzzle his nape.

Let go and let love baby.

The hall didn't collapse. No one vomited. We weren't asked to leave, nor stoned to death. No epithets were hurled. No one exited in disgust that I know of.

We were lucky.

Another responded to my cousin's disgust, "This is family. If it can't happen here, where else?"

No need to escape that night, rush off to a gay bar. For one stardust shining moment before midnight, we danced, in love. With family.

Don Pyle. My prince. My heart. I could've danced all night.

Or, as my Fairy Godmother in *Cinderella* sings, "Impossible things can happen every day."

She Left

"Do not buy into their system of censorship, imagining that if you drop this character or hide that emotion, you can slide through their blockades. Do not eat your heart out in the hope of pleasing them."

—Dorothy Allison,
"Survival is the Least of My Desires"

During Reagan's landslide she knew
"I have no future in this country."

O, to be Carrie White.

The tears, the thoughts to say anything meant certain destruction.
(She meant years…)

To obliterate themself, or the entire room?
(Or the entire room and themself?)

> "We would rather be ruined than changed;
> We would rather die in our dread
> Than climb the cross of the moment
> And let our illusions die"
>
> —W.H. Auden

The American Way
football to Armageddon
on speed dial

What panics Americans most? Difference.

"Precisely, baby," Baldwin exhaling smoke.

Our Friendly Murderers.

I'm not Canadian by default. It's by choice.
Came for schooling. Met a fella. Fell in love.

She wanted to live their life this lifetime.
Not some other "promised" life.

Who will tend their mother's grave?

Krogering

"Let's go Krogering" jingles on the speakers. My mother Suzanne and I have the same look on our faces, eyeing the same ginger at checkout bagging our goods.

"Ask him out," she nudges.

"WTF? MOM! We're at fucking KROGER'S and he's working" as I move to walk the cart towards the exit…

"O, no," she stops me, "He'll do that, they do that here."

"It's okay, Mom," rushing for the exit, thinking she's behind me.

Loading bags into the car, she hands me a slip.

"His name is Daniel. Here's his number."

I look at her.

"What? He's got a job and there's good benefits at Kroger. You'll never go hungry."

"Yeah, but he is gay?"

"You got his number. Call him."

"You call him."

"He's too young for me."

"All Great Truths Begin as Blasphemies."

—George Bernard Shaw,
Annajanska, The Bolshevik Empress

What adamant "heterosexual rights" zealots and a couple of self-hating "ex-gays" always fail to understand is that the only choice people make regarding their sexual proclivities is whether or not to make them public. And what isn't public these days? Only the religious/conservative marrying-kind still insist on getting caught in lies (a turn-on, apparently). For them, their private parts remain a private matter, and we already know what sorts of things go on in private. And why it remains so. It's "don't ask, don't tell" every day of their chosen, church-goin', secretive lives. And if it's good for them, it ought to be good for everyone, right? No "special rights." Their sacred cow—marriage (American-style)—is only for one man and one woman to fuck up. Many times over. Thank you, Lord. Things are just fine the way they are as long as the faithful (read: unquestioning) pray to God and pretend not to know about the things they don't want others, especially the children or the neighbours, to know about.

Lies are far more interesting, juicy—beg to be told/ revealed—often playfully served up with glee. We love our lies. Relish our truth in them. Expect them. "Told you so." The truth itself? Not so much. Who cares. The truth may indeed at times prevail, but it's the lies we want exposed.

As journalist Gerald Hannon once said, "It's your lies I want. I already know your truths."

In lies we trust. They're a whole lot easier to swallow. Ultra-palatable. And o so believable. Feed me another. Something dishy. Especially about so-and-so.

No! He's not! You're making that up! Really?! We're not surprised.

America's obesity: one big fat lie sweetly served and swallowed after another.

No Contest

"What does it mean to be a citizen of a country on the wrong side of every liberation struggle on this earth?"

—Audre Lorde

America
you can
not will not
win   there is
no fucking "win"
no finish
no free billions
trillions
made in China
O, the savings!
the minute
your first million-dollar
grunt touches boot
upon their soil
One giant step
you expect them
to greet rollover
who wouldn't want
these Walmart prices

entering
plundering
destroying devastating
all
in the name of
your Almighty
American interests
taking pocketing
FAILING
One big obese
"F"
as in
FUCK YOU
homeless jobless penniless
FUCK YOU
diseased infected
gays illegals
as in
hell-bent mother
fucking Dick
Cheney
seeing stars stripes
forever
corn-holy
FUCKED.

Haggard

To say I have no empathy for closeted televangelist Ted Haggard would place me alongside his more religious, vengeful, unforgiving followers who defrocked and banished him from his own New Life [Mega] Church in Colorado.

This is, first and foremost, a story about how the Church treats its own. Not a new story. Gays have been killed, wished dead, tossed out of their families for centuries. Not in the name of Christ, but in the name of whatever evil, authoritarian church/state executes power over our bodies.

If Christ is a liberator, nobody told American evangelicals.

This is also the age-old story of living the double life of a liar. Ted Haggard clearly had good reasons to lie. I mean, all gays know they've got to lie to live, let alone to get anywhere in this world. This is "I believe marriage is between one man and one woman" (in successive attempts) America. You don't want people to know you're gay. To find out. Not your family. Not your employer. Not your church. I mean, you just know what they'll do to you. They'll strip you. You'll lose everything.

They'll crucify you. (Again, not a new story).

I don't know Mr. Haggard. We've never met outside of his rather sizable media reach. Based on his television persona alone, this is not a man I would seek to share closeness with or befriend. To me, he puts the snake in snake oil. Still, he got tens of thousands, perhaps millions, to believe in his lie. Not the truth in Christ that sets the captive free, but the lie that you can't be a man and lie down with another man and live freely, openly, to tell the story.

You can't be gay like Jesus.

(O Mary, don't ask.)

So, once again, we have a story of a man who cheated, duped his family, parishioners, and told countless gay kids to "fight the good fight" (or die trying). He sold an empty bag of goods, quotable sound bites, biblical gumdrops to cherry-picked tow-the-hardline believers who never falter in their beliefs… but are always caught in the lie.

Ted, I don't blame you for lying. For believing your lies. For becoming a top of the game "truth pedlar." There's some unique, albeit disingenuous, craft in that.

And, I don't blame you for so badly wanting to be straight. For continuing to sit in the same pew with people who would compare you to murderers. Lower than murderers. Hitler. Scum. Exiling you and your family to perish. Fend for yourselves.

Hell, I'd even forgive you for denying Christ a third time. You can live in denial for the rest of your god-given life insurance selling days.

But, I'll never forgive the intentional harm you caused your own cockbreathed kind. I'd never ask even one of my gay (or non-gay) sisters, brothers, to pick up their nets to follow you.

She Left 2

It's one of those mornings that I just don't have it in me.

Sure, I'm up, the coffee is made, the sink is emptied and cleaned, breakfast is prepped and into the oven, and I've committed to an outing this aft. I'd cancel in a heartbeat though, and I'm still not certain how or if I'll get there.

Motions, baby. E-minus.

Missed my sister's call. Expect ice storm in the next hour.

All this and a lil more before my first sip of Italian roast at 10:24am. The data doesn't actually match, line-up with, this all-pervasive "feeling."

I simply don't want to be here any longer.

Sit down to a k-zillion things I could should be doing… and individually, it's all somewhat worthwhile. But when I'm lie this (meant to read like, but lie is interesting…), it's hard to differentiate, all one big clusterfuck of "yeah, yeah I know, I'll get to it."

(Maybe not.)

Nothing's hard. I mean there is no real "hardship," to speak of. Things will get done or they won't.

It's not like I'm in a state where others will decide if I live or not.

Two National Guardsman miles from home, ("you must not follow illegal orders" = "SEDITIOUS BEHAVIOR, punishable by DEATH!"), on patrol doing just that... shot by an Afghan national. American Thanksgiving eve.

How does one carry a hate over centuries that can blow a city's guts out?

Maybe it was just a bad day. SMITHEREENS!

Poke me with a stick, I feel nothing. Nothing carefree or hopeful in this world.

We've seen it all before. Predictable as their ALL MAN response.

A wannabe with a sharpie calls them "animals." The guardsmen, "losers."

These measly-ass replies:

"This isn't who we are." (Show me otherwise, fuckers.)

"CALL UP FIVE-HUNDRED MORE ON DUTY."

"THIS WILL NOT STAND."

One friend calls Thanksgiving "reprehensible," sitting down to a feast while there's a genocide (paired with mourning the loss of his beloved).

Why is the measure of love loss?

To sit with his loss.

Hers. Theirs. And theirs.

Another posts a video on how it's fucking hard, frightening, to go outside, leave the house.

Expect rain in the next hour.

"Doesn't mean everyone has to stop. Fuck them."

Friend responding to this news:

"THE US GOVERNMENT WILL NOT BE RECOGNIZING WORLD AIDS DAY THIS YEAR."

They can't even commemorate our losses. Loved ones.

Family in the States: pictures of cooked birds, holiday cheer.

Dig my body out of this avalanche first. (She's dead. Never mind.)

Never once wishing the same ("Canadian Thanksgiving? What's that? That's not real Thanksgiving.")

"Gay marriage?! That's not real." (Must've been a slow news day, she adds).

What's that smell?

FUCK!

Italian Wedding soup. Left on the burner. Who the fuck burns a can of Italian Wedding soup?

Google: "Floaters."

"For every 20 minutes of computer viewing, look into the distance for 20 seconds to allow the eyes a chance to refocus."

Look out.

They lied. It's snow.

Jeanette

"A tough life needs a tough language—and that's what poetry is. That is what literature offers—a language powerful enough to say how it is."

—Jeanette Winterson,
Why Be Happy When You Could Be Normal?

Jeanette Winterson has saved my life countless times/reads. Her *Written on the Body* is a classic.

"Why is the measure of love loss?" Something I feel with every pore of my being.

When's the last time a book has caused you to swoon? Want? More?

Seeing/hearing all 5'6" of her in a packed sanctuary (Trinity Church behind the Eaton Centre) was like having a comet crash into the pews.

How rare for someone/anyone to match/exceed my joy. Honest to goddess, a human vibrator.

"CLEAR!" Paddles zapping, my chest heaving, SHE'S ALIVE!

Winterson: "How many of us ever get free of our orbit?"

We collectively don't even watch films together anymore.

Go outside? Fuck that noise.

Go to a poetry reading (knowing full well the poets themselves don't even want to be there, and leave before the next reader)?

Go to a bar where everybody just sits there… on their phones?

Canadian publishers imploring everyone to BUY CANADIAN thinking that might somehow move their brand spanking new unsold titles. ("Nothing is selling." Cause people can't afford it or no longer care).

RuPaul's hologram: "READING IS WHAT?!"

"D I S P O S A B L E!!!" the queens on Drag Race Antarctica season 69 squeal!

Perhaps if you started selling disposable pads/tablets downloaded with your new season.

Make mine PRO.

"Books will come back."

Yeah, like vinyl that costs $100 bucks. Limited pink edition.

What's the next outrageously expensive thing everyone will go into debt for?

"Expect sleet in the next hour."

She can't afford a bomb as big as their enemy. Hurry up Global Warming.

Never mind. Spin the globe. On the eve of AI, we're good as dead.

Winterson: "I try not to burn up my world with rage. It is so hard."

I can't lift my own weight.

All I can do is dry cry.

Almost forgot. Buy Canadian.

Kirby: "How many of you have been called 'faggot' on the streets of London?"

More than half the room raise their hands.

Kirby: "Thanks for coming out tonight."

Nothing is more essential then having spaces free from violence where we can gather, love, play, celebrate.

"It's all about the lighting," Kirby smiles.

The Good

Pardoned felons, ex-cops, 18+ paid a $50K
bonus to sign-up, kill their own people

in their own neighbourhoods
down the street from where they live,

attend mass, call themselves Christian
and call everyone else "fucking bitch."

Herself, a believer
married, kids, more guiltless

good in her taxpayer pinky then the whole
lawless lot of Botox-driven millions

of Christ's own each and every
minute of each and every day.

"What a beautiful job our military did
[insert illegal war here]."

"I'm not mad at you." Renee. To the ICE guard.
Last seen. Smiling.

Being Silly

Bright crisp Sunday morning.

"The chicken was juicy and delicious. A keeper!" (My inbox).

Goodness. Who doesn't want, (or want to be), that chicken!

Smart call clearing the balcony yesterday, covering the AC, bringing the plants in, staging the living room, welcoming a fresh oxygen source, though bittersweet. Life is infinitely better (mentally/physically) during months the balcony is open, with my lil perch view of Church Street and the Village shared mostly one-on-one with poets, familiars. A lifesaver in peak COVID lockdown—it felt like being out on the street, or just going out period at a time when so much stinking thinking was warped in isolation.

Am I hanging a string of lights this year? The same all-orange strand that's bathed my winter nights the past decade (could be two)—big non-LED bulbs I rarely come across at Canadian Tire, always picking up what they have on hand for spares.

It's not that I'm Christmassy, but the lights always remind me of lit theatre marquees and neon… "What's playing?" They thrill me with expectancy, still.

This year, I just want to keep the dark at bay.

On my mother Suzanne's final visit here, she spotted me from a stool as we screwed in bulbs to see which ones still lit, flicking them with our fingernails, pocketing dead ones to be tossed. A couple of boys below voiced their disdain loud enough, "I hate it."

"Pay no mind to them," Suzanne said, handing me a new orange one from the packet, so happy to be of help. I reach, "Be careful!" she says, "Here… got it?"

"I just love the orange, you can light these for Halloween."

Gorgeous light fixtures the boys (Joseph & Leo) continue to find me are also present, cast orange warmth. I find most people look good in this light. Kind to the skin, the eyes. Glowing.

There's a Toronto blue sky. Late October. Autumn blue.

Couples of all-sorts stroll up and down Church (lots of actual strollers, baby and two wheelers hovering above the street). Dozens of new buildings erect new families. Athletic types slog big-ass bags full of hockey equipment—"girl, you're pushing it in those shorts!"

Frank Sinatra sings "Just in Time" on JAZZ FM 91.1 from *Bells Are Ringing*, a musical I played comic relief in at Rogers High School (circa 1975), as some wacky dentist who sings an equally silly "The Midas Touch."

The funny fella, the fag, not the lead. She delivered. Made it memorable. Werk.

> Just in time, I found you just in time
> Before you came my time was running low
> I was lost, the losing dice were tossed
> My bridges all were crossed, no where to go
> Now you're here, now I know just where I'm going
>
> No more doubt or fears I've found my way
> For love came just in time
>
> You found me just in time
> And changed my lonely life that lucky day
>
> —Jule Styne,
> Adolph Green, Betty Comden

Damn, I've got to throw on a sweater.

Reading tonight. Guesting in support of poets David Bateman and Stedmond Pardy and their (ongoing) pet project *Two Voices for Tennessee Williams*, hard to picture an odder, sweeter pairing (*Midnight Cowboy* comes lovingly to mind). Their real affinity for Tenn and each other shines and I'm humbled by an invite to coalesce in their living homage of a treasured homosexual icon at none other than the legendary Imperial Pub, soon to be swallowed whole by Toronto Metropolitan University (an entity that is also re-branding Dundas Station and the public square. Money honey.)

My own writings got a reboot upstairs in the "Library Lounge" at the pub decades ago when Hoa Nguyen and Dale Smith hosted a workshop with CAConrad, a dive with only one operable washroom (gender-neutral that day, skirted figure on the door!) and some of the last great original neon signage in the downtown core.

Sofonda Tennessee (my drag name?). Starmaker. Starbreaker. Brando's wife-beater. Taylor's smoke. Geraldine Page's gin. Someone everybody wanted to work with… until they didn't.

They can't all be "Streetcars," but there was desire, always, in buckets.

The falsities of hetero living: lonely boys and girls hard on their heels, a taste of the big time coming up short.

Success and failure baby. Luck or you're down a few quarts. Or worse.

A shortlist of the (publicly/commercial) famous homosexual playwrights/writers of the time: Albee, Baldwin, Capote, Genet?, Rechy, Vidal, Williams. As long as they were successful, made the producers/ publishers their profits. A string of bad notices were tantamount to losing everything. Reduced to faggotry, a common criminal.

Yes, please.

One must be wanted. In some way or other. Beloved alcohol, shady lover. The kindness of strangers.

I read Williams' *Memoirs* when they first appeared in 1975, as an out homosexual myself at the ripe age of 15. Courageous? Brave? No darlins, she was a fairy. There was no "in" (except for being funny—Paul Lynde, Charles Nelson Reilly, Harvey Fierstein—then only laughably excusable).

What a gift, these tellings. A man desiring men. Staying afloat. Alive. I now live for this quaint demure telling:

There were two very beautiful young men who acted in a play at the University Theatre […] one […] made a screen debut in a film based on the life of Valentino. He had a fantastically perfect body. The other beautiful young actor […] asked me to have dinner with him one night—he was troubled over something, he said, and he didn't know how to tell me what it was. But after a few beers he did.

"Y'know I went in [his] bedroom last night and he was there naked and I—well, I—I don't know how to tell you but I felt something like I wanted to touch him like a man does a woman, y'know."

He kept his long-lashed eyes on the table. His face beautifully flushed […]

When I finally spoke I said to him, "There's nothing about it to be upset over."

"It isn't a natural thing," he whispered.

"Yes it is," I said. "It's a perfectly natural thing and you're just being silly."

I walked him home to his dormitory
and we shook hands goodnight.

"Fantastically perfect body." "The other beautiful young actor." "Troubled." "Long-lashed." "Flushed." "Y'know."

"You're just being silly."

What a perfectly adept sweet loving response.

Music to my Fairy, my romantic never been kissed queer teenage lips.

The laughter between me and my kind. Teach me Tennessee.

WUSS

Fag for Hire

Job Interview. First question.

Client: "I know I'm not supposed to, but I gotta ask, are you gay?"

Manager steps in: "You know you're not allowed to ask that."

I get it, young bloke with a spinal cord injury in need of attendant care, dressing, undressing, showering, assisting with bowel movements, a condom on his penis for urine. Meals. 7/24. Daily. Why should he have to put up with some faggot in his home touching him?

"It's okay, I can answer. Yes, fortunately for you, I am homosexual. One of the reasons so many homosexuals are drawn to the service field is that, given our lived experience, we tend to care about how others are treated with dignity and respect. Nothing less."

"I hope you find someone as worthy, dedicated, and professional to fill this position."

Stand. Exit.

(She took the job.)

The Ripple in Your Flag

"We pledge allegiance to the fag."

—Kevin Killian

Maybe because it was a flag. Maybe because the flag was placed pretty much everywhere—first to designate gay businesses, then every business wanting gay patronage. It was supposed to express support for diversity, the colours of the rainbow (now, even more inclusive, the OG skipped a few hues), at best a designated safe spot: "Olly olly oxen free!"

I must say, the Trans Flag *is* pretty, with its elemental, simple, soft colour palette.

"You're IT!" "Un-HUH! You can't get me here! This is home base."

To touch a tree, foot on the bag, run, hide beneath the porch, the tall grasses.

"HOME FREEEEEEEEEEEEEEE!"

You know why they're pissed. The gays up and ruined their kid's bible story, you know the one, with

God sending Noah a rainbow as a promise and a sign, that they would never flood the world again ("Raise the rainbow flag Gilligan!" "Sure thing, Skipper!").

Sorry, is it he or they? Another reason why they're dishevelled. God forbid you give them more than one choice.

O, that and marriage. The gays spoiled that too.

Their darlin' child Kevin enters bustin' their best duck walk then body drops—all gleaned from their favourite queens on Mama Ru…

"No fair! No fair! You keep changing the rules!" "No I'm not, YOU are!"

Pretty much everything they ever needed to know learned on that playground. Who your friends are (for the hour anyway). The bullies. Boys. Girls. Mostly separate. The ones who play fair, cheat when no one's looking. Get caught.

Is it still cheating if no one cares? If no one notices the beaten, detained, killed?

"I didn't see a thing. I won't tell nobody. Promise." BAM! Dead. Every Netflix film.

Disappeared. Silenced. No reason. A tyrant. A whim.

"It's them. They're the ones who don't belong."

They/them.

Me. My people.

Once called, "The third sex."

"BIG SHOW TONIGHT! SPECIAL GUEST: MR. RECORDER!" and they would pre-tape the answers to the "live" questions on their reel-to-reel played for anybody who showed up in the living room.

"Julie, Julie, Julie do you love me?"!!! My youngest sister HATING that song. They dreamed of Bobby Sherman, all teeth, hair, and flairs (my Farrah Fawcett), being their friend (not David Soul, "too manly.")

Not Robin… (there already was one). They wanted to be "Little Batman." And only we did things, Batman and me (WITHOUT Robin. Same with Johnny Quest).

What they didn't know is they were always out. Loud. Couldn't help it if their life depended on it.

But, as long as nobody said anything… (most of all, them).

Fairy didn't know enough not to be "too." Hilarious. (A BIG FAT "F" circled in pink).

They were supposed to be "fighting the good fight," transitioning into being straight. "M."

The mother of a friend even mailed me a lovely note, imploring me to "fight the good fight…"

Girl. Wtf? That sounds like your fight. Not mine.

Can there please, please be a different story? (Pretty please?)

This one (that of the oppressed) is tired. The fight. The struggle. Lifetimes tired. Generations tired. "Am I just repeating myself here?" Preaching the gospel. There are things worth putting on repeat ("Your silence will not protect you." Audre Lorde), but never let that get in the way of a fresh shuffle. New. Ground. (Gay plants!)

They've aged. But, still here for it. The realness.

It's just history repeating. White Christian Nationalists try to make more babies to catch up, not slip into a "minority."

Not everyone sees (or welcomes) fairies. Not even gays. Children do. My Fairy is "The Fairy of Delicates," not the most masculine version of gay, or as my nephew said once they connected the dots, "You're just like Jack on *Will & Grace*!" He could be wrong, but still, I love his joy in seeing me. Being recognized as one of them.

Who is they now? Them? The Other? (Remember that big Tom Tryon horror novel turned into creepy 70s film with John Ritter?).

Othering. The opposite of inclusion. The monied. Everyone else.

This othering is so other than me, maybe because I spent a lifetime seeing/seeking likes. Reflectors. Today, I'm just as "othered" by my aging. My obesity. My poverty and shifting disabilities.

Human stuff. The daily.

Poet Frank Bidart wrote a brilliant lil gem, "Queer." Here's the opening stanza:

> Lie to yourself about this and you will
> forever lie about everything.

Everybody already knows everything

so you can
lie to them. That's what they want.

But lie to yourself, what you will

lose is yourself. Then you
turn into them.

Turning into them. Yes, that's what my enemies want (still/forever) more than anything (okay, face it, they really want us dead). No ripples to conformity. No body nothing but what their "God" deems "correct."

"Red light. Fuck it. LET'S GO!"

I am the fold in your flag, not the flag, the ripple, flapping trans colours, snapping the wind.

And today, this day, I live. Other. Victor victorious. Pride baby. Pride.

A Fag's Life

May there never be a time my face
doesn't reek of your pits, balls.

The stuff of real life

1.

Living my whole life as though I was keeping some deep dark secret.

To this moment. Today.

What I've been doing is what I've learned my whole fairy life.

Well, not my whole life… the day my Fairy was called a "fairy"—

since then.

Check the room constantly. Make certain it's okay for me to be

here, my thoughts filtered by whether I can

register any motion movement

signs of threat openness

absence disappointment.

So rarely is my Fairy met in kind.

You can tell when somebody sees you

yes?

With welcome

yes?

Internalized Homophobia?

How horribly categorically redundantly adult.

So unfairylike.

No. This is something else.

Fairy knows.

I'm a sprite

flesh and blood, this life

craving to be the breeze

an oak shapeshifting

between worlds lives

simply to show

this too is possible.

2.

To name things
as though that's

what they are
is helpful at times

when agreed upon

My Fairy's favourite
thing is to queer all

that is silly
strait-laced.

She's a fairy
after all.

3.

"Nature is busy creating
Absolutely unique
Individuals, whereas culture
Has invented a *single mold*
To which all must conform.
It is grotesque."

—Michael Pollan

How does she know

she is not these

flowers? Accurate

reflectors as she

finishes this puff.

Why Get Up?

When the breeze from a ceiling fan hits
their thighs just so on an August morning

She can cook. She can clean.
She pours a lovely bubble bath!

Their new drag name:
"Cum Bubble."

Writing still guard-railed in my mind.
By them. Still. At it.

Some call it "fucked up."
I call it home.

"Girl. Where the fuck's your broom?
Get up. There's cleaning to do."

Never Assume Wrong

"We understand the world better if we tremble with it."

—Édouard Glissant

Most temples I have entered "unknowingly,"

my Fairy's queer predilection.

You never know when you're going to enter

a temple

the slurp ramp at the Bijou

desire path behind Allen Gardens

the dumpster at Varsity Arena

Philosopher's Walk

dormie cock through chain link fence

cheer from their windows

Trinity College

the loo at Byzantium

an apartment garage stairwell

the pillars of the memorial

second floor University Hall

the magic bushes at Cherry Beach

limbs rise Queen's park

the worn path along the crick

trees to recline against in repose

the paradise that was the perfect

sex palace Jorgenson Hall Scotia Plaza

fourth floor between classes NYU

above the Lillian Gish theatre

second floor porn set of stalls U of M

ducking behind a piece of plywood

Christopher Street

the Cathedral at PITT

this perfect little spot, a men's room

tucked beneath a stairwell Gillam Hall

behind the curtains of Doermann U of T

Menjo's parking lot in a car in the rain

the Las Vegas Cinema next door to the Open Closet

Steak & Fags on Central

late nights at the Eastwood, Westwood

filling stations converted to busy peeps

on the way to work, lunch hour, breaks

a quick stop before your home life,

when the bars close and everybody wants

a lil something.

This is Fairy's queer movement. Monument.
Moment.

May “queers” and “fucking” be the keyword search for Kirby.

“Just a girlyboy with a praise kink seeking idols.”

Total idolatry. Each setting, the stench of spunk.

Men.

A tender thumb wipes the wet from my cheeks.

“Good Cocksucker.”

Trans

"No insurgent intellectual, no dissenting critical voice in this society escapes the pressure to conform [...] we are all vulnerable. We can all be had, co-opted, bought. There is no special grace that rescues any of us. There is only constant struggle."

—bell hooks

"Kirby, you do know you're trans."

"Say more."

My first "transitioning" was trying to be a man.

No one was buying it.

I, for one, was the last to know how girlish(?) I was/am.

What measuring tape do we use? Does one measure one's "effeminacy?"

Constantly being told not to be so loud,

when I wasn't any loader than those noisemakers

around me. My voice stood out

became yet another means to be targeted.

Crazy insistence of homogeny.

She was effusive as she was sensitive.

Their first art project (kindergarten?)

she took up the chain stitch, hand sewed a big

green dragon gifted to Suzanne who attached it to a pillow

placed it on the living room sofa. So fine.

That must be somewhere, god knows she wouldn't

just toss it out. (O, she does toss, just not this.)

No one can "tell you" you're trans / however you choose to identify.

We're in constant transition. Is there anything more human?

My preferred title is non-binary which I understand falls

under the Trans umbrella—shades of pink, baby blue.

I'm happy to carry, share

with likes in need of shelter from the elements.

Pants

"If I'm wearing pants, call me a man. If I'm wearing a dress, call me a cab!"

—Holly Woodlawn

Holly and I "came out" at the same ripe young age of fifteen. Like many queers she ran away from home to the Big Apple only to become an iconic fixture at Warhol's Factory, cast in Paul Morrissey 70's classic, *Trash* (opposite my one true flame, Joe Dallesandro), and immortalized by the Lou Reed song "Walk on the Wild Side."

My first transition was becoming a man, not because I wanted to be one, but because I had a standard issue penis and it seemed that to attract the men I sought, I learned to butch it up a bit. I know, laughable, but I was furry and for a while could pull off a tank top and boxers. Lord, what a boy has to do to attract men. (Right "ladies?") It was SO much easier simply to be gay, and how does one measure the right amount of gaiety?

I mean, I truly didn't realize exactly how gay I was, and/or why the fuck that should ever matter. EV-VAH.

She played the clarinet ffs. "Strike!"

Let's simply say, in those days those considered on the more effeminate side were often frowned upon. Still are.

"Big Queen" had yet to reach the level of fabulousness it enjoys today.

It always makes me laugh, the idea of acting too gay—you know, the kind of limp-wristed fey that straights (or even gays) strike in a pose, buckling over in laughter as they overact some chichéd gesture of being a pansy.

"Strike two!"

The best men for me are never afraid of busting out their big girl.

There's a whole lotta fucked up history that says boys and girls, women and men, should stay in their lane, behave in a particular way. Gendered.

And yet, it's never ever been that way.

Not even in prisons.

They say, "be true to yourself."

"STRIKE THREE!"

Okay, I'm a criminal. At least, I was then.

Genet, Rechy, Pasolini taught me to go the way of the criminal.

It doesn't matter that the powers that be hate you.

They only love power. And, when I dance to Kylie,

they have no power over me. None.

The glories of being fey.

Yes, Langston. She's tired.

"It is exhausting, living in a population where people don't speak up if what they witness doesn't directly threaten them."

—David Wojnarowicz

"How many genders are there?"

"How many push-ups can you do?"

"My rocket is bigger than yours."

"Here's a million dollars for your party this weekend
Mr. President."

Yes, Langston, she's tired.

She's read Beckett

heeded his laugh

be it one of terror

catastrophe dismay.

What exactly are we waiting for?

The bombs, the fires, the waters
the messiah the lack of
real cheese eggs bread butter
mayo. She's spoiled.
Fairy knows what tastes
served sparingly on holidays
special occasions. Who feeds
the trillionaires? Do they eat
differently then the billionaires?
Certainly the poor millionaires
suffer but for only $19 a month
(that's only 63 cents a day)
you can help a feed/clothe
a child in need rescue an animal
from the freezing cold fight
for reproductive rights equal

rights LGBTQ rights stop the banning
of books ("in LIBRARIES,"
Judy Blume exclaims) perhaps you need
a chair lift hearing aids something
for your prostate leaking underwear
two-hundred uses there must be some
on 45/47's webstore "Make America
Dry Again" mmmmaybe not? Men don't
wear protection unless in combat
only women need protection.
All-body deodorants, I can't believe
I lived with that stank all this
time the lord giveth
and the lord taketh away Poof!
"My home is gone." Poof!
"My job, gone." Poof!

Family, loved ones

eyesight ability to walk gone

a child opens their hands

"all gone!" covers their face

"all gone!" places an empty dish

on their head "all gone!"

For just $10 a month

(that's just 33 cents a day)

My Lorde

"I want to live the rest of my life, however long or short, with as much sweetness as I can decently manage, loving all the people I love, and doing as much as I can of the work I still have to do. I am going to write fire until it comes out of my ears, my eyes, my nose holes—everywhere. Until it's every breath I breathe. I'm going to out like a fucking meteor!"

—Audre Lorde

Audre Lorde is the kind of fucking rudder it takes to get through these waters—hell, to even get up in the morning.

Not sorry-ass whining over every piddly thing big or small that sieves through social media.

There is no community, no sustenance to be found there. Branded pitches, people trolling for attention, praying you'll pause, favour a "like" (better still, a sale), hours on end til everything's but a blip.

The internet is yet another sneaky way to make us dependent. No wonder we scroll on something called a feed.

"Open wide."

Only now, we've added AI so you won't even have a job to keep you from your Beloved. Scroll baby scroll.

Anything to further dumb down the masses. Hold us captive.

Schools no longer require students to read (whole) books anymore, library books largely remain untouched (except for maybe the banned ones).

Why retain anything when you can simply bark orders/question your personal device/assistant?

"It's a lot quicker than trying to google it."

Quicker than Google? To find out if so and so is gay, or married, or how much they're worth?

"Many people find it helpful to discuss their personal life with ChatGPT."

I googled it.

Now, I know any or all of this way of thinking is simply laughable, made even more so at the time of your reading (or hearing, or however you're digesting this book).

Fucking AI (and yes I do mean literally) will become as common as… let's say heterosexuality (a dying concept according to Christian fascists).

First query: "Chatty?"

"Yes, darlin'?"

"Is heterosexuality common in Canada, the US?"

"Well of course it is silly! Not everybody can be fabulous like you!"

"Awwwww, shugr, you're just trying to butter me up."

"Just tell me you're not like my last zillion tricks, all they want is a quickie… I felt nothing. Not a thing. Like he wasn't there."

"Sounds like reading a [fill in blank] poem."

"Exactly."

#SSS*

"So to you straight folks, I say—sure, I'll go, if you go too. But I'm polite—so after you."

—Pat Parker

Humourless fucking straight shit is the only thing I find truly tiresome.

But, I'm polite.

* Stupid Straight Shit

Omg. She went out.

Sunday. Retro night. Black Eagle.

Brendon at the bar, “Welcome back.”

Bud in hand, I head to the dance floor.

“You’ve got to show me love.”

Dance, baby dance.

Lovely boy beside me knocks into me twice,

“I’m sorry, I’m so clumsy,” smiles.

Me, “Enjoy.”

Beautiful shirtless bearded boy, the form I came out for

“I normally listen to this in my living room.”

“Music of my whole life baby.”

“You know where this is going…”

Groove is in the heart, sadly cut off too soon.

“I could’ve listened to Deee-Lite all night.”

Omg, he moves in close—

“My name is Kirby.”

"Herbie?"

“No, Kirby with a K.”

“Hello Kirby with a K,” smiles, wraps his arms around me.

“Thanks for your sweetness.”

“O, there’s plenty of that.”

She laughs, “I’m already drowning!”

Grabs my hand, takes me to the floor.

“You remind me of Marky Mark, only a man.”

Laughs “A Man?” He scoops me up in his arms

off my feet (girl practically shrieked)!

When's the last time my feet

left the floor? My prince.

On the way out, Patricia and I hug goodnight. Love her.

fairy

Hello Stranger

"If you cannot live the life / you long for, do your best / not to lessen the life you have."

—C.P. Cavafy,
"As Best You Can,"
translated by Evan Jones

Can she do another round? Does she even want to?

"How *are* you?" and/or, "Are you *okay*?"

(For real?!) "Where are the washrooms?"

Of course it matters who's asking. Too often it's someone who imagines a relationship closer than the one we share, to which my silent response is, "none of your business."

My mom Suzanne would ask about things. My reply, "Are you sure you want to know the answer?" ("Maybe not." "I'd tell you mom." "No. You wouldn't." Laughter.)

I can tell you. I'm not doing well. And, I can tell you exactly why I'm not doing well:

Because the world is less and less recognizable to me, beginning with the streets where I live. Not only do I not feel safe, I'm not safe (especially on the TTC, which is unforgivable). It's hard enough to get around. I muster and manage as called upon. It's a courageous act (not a gift) to continue. She repeats herself. I know.

"I'm not happy."

Suzanne would say, "So what?"

I don't like where this is going and I'm tired of being a complainer on shuffle ("walk from pelvis, lift your knees.") Adding to the growing chorus of groaners who may in fact have reason, I'd rather not.

I have food on my table and a roof over my head. Loving friends who invite/care. She's surrounded by beauty. A stunning new poetry collection out. Why do I feel destitute?

Well, for one thing, I am.

I'm still getting out from under debt just shy of swallowing me whole. Reaganomics killed my father (well, that and a carton of smokes a week). Thirty-plus years in sheet metal suddenly gone belly-up, bankrupt. He couldn't see his way out of it either.

He was so lost he told me standing in the garage he'd sooner be dying from AIDS. While I knew that was some serious stinking thinking, I understood he'd hit bottom and was seeking an exit. It's not always the actual virus that kills.

I am now six years older than my dad.

I am heartbroken daily. So much loss. Too much. The burning world. This bitter earth.

I cannot live the life I long for, and while I'm doing my best to continue, it's not my first impulse. Life has finally (yet, again) knocked me on my ass.

I've made a practice of practicing ease ("How might this be easier?") for decades, only because my early years romanticized "the struggle." Life is not easy for homosexuals. Now, there's actual struggle. Or have I circled back to that default approach in search of a familiar?

Suzanne, "You don't want to grow old."

And he drags himself to the cafés all day long, drags the weariness consuming his beauty. - @cavafybot

Where are the exits?

Cavafy detested aging, a vanity (understandable) accompanied by an acknowledgement that his sustenance was found midst the temples of men. A life of chosen servitude, devotion. I know, lived it well. My adoring eyes haven't changed one iota, a high beam that remains on full, a willing satellite.

I know I can do things differently. And I know not to wait around to "feel like it." Decisions to be made (like it or not). Easier to take the walk than ponder it to death. No, she doesn't want to. ("I can't go on. I go on.") She can be a stubborn pretty Taurus.

Then, there's that last line of Cavafy's:

"life is not a tiresome stranger."

And a tiresome stranger seems to have visited upon me. Taken up residence somehow. Pandemic leftovers? It may be death (I'm not afraid, my wish/want has never been longevity). I may in fact have one more round left in me. I can even (barely) begin to make out the leap involved. A stirring. (Or just gas! Laughter. There she is. Her belly.)

The will to do something completely different. May we all find it.

Meanwhile, salvation is at hand. The new Pet Shop Boys, *Nonetheless* (their fifteenth studio album) is nothing less than brilliant. Sublime and just in time. Dance stars, dance.

Here's the full poem by Cavafy (translated by Evan Jones):

As Best You Can

If you cannot live the life
you long for, do your best
not to lessen the one you have
with mundane distractions
with posturing and gossip.

Do not lessen it by taking hold,
turning around and exposing it
to relationships that wallow
in everyday nonsense:
life is not a tiresome stranger.

Fuck important

"You should read this! It's important!" Might as well be junk mail… straight to recycle.

Nobody likes to be told. I can decide what's important to me, thank you very much.

There was a string drawer at my grandma's stuffed so full it took my entire body weight to pull it open even a little bit, and I would spend the day untangling, sorting through threads, either winding them onto a wooden spool, or into a ball. For her. O the colours! Nothing brought me more joy. (Okay, she also taught how to bread and pan-fry pork chops, also life changing).

Reconnecting with an old friend from university days, my first "diva," a gorgeous singer, photographer, cultural historian who now has a Substack mostly centred around bric-a-brac, embroideries, buttons, finds in sewing boxes—you know, the good stuff. What enchants.

I shared my love for my friend's site while she was still hemming and hawing over whether or not she should start asking for paid subscriptions, and yes, I said, it's a wonderful niche world you've created and certainly of the calibre for paying readers. Still, she wondered.

"I mean my stuff's about knick-knacks, your writing is so important, necessary."

"O, yours is too" I replied. "Do you think for a second I want the stuff I write about to be in any way important? I'd much rather be posting pictures of my grandmother's button jars."

"Your site is an oasis. Where I come for respite." Subscribed.

As to what I was being told I should read before, hmm. I forget. Guess it wasn't all that.

Does every book have to be laden with a MESSAGE?

Fairy winks, "maybe." Blows a kiss.

How to Get Published

My first full-length poetry collection, *This Is Where I Get Off*, was published by Matt Finner at Permanent Sleep Press in 2019.

I had just turned 60.

Here's how it happened:

There were attempts at an earlier version of the book called *Drunk on Cock*. Local artist Leo Scopacasa designed a killer cover, and graphic designer Randy McPhee, who collaborated on earlier fliers for my Queer Sex Stories reading series and "Sex is Not the Enemy" talks, worked his magic on the layout. I was even inviting investors to have a Kirby-cooked dinner with me at my home to raise funds for a new publishing venture, Anus Press, with a Vonnegut-like asshole asterisk as the logo.

(I remember someone telling me at the time, re: the press name, "you know Kirby, the literary world takes their presses very seriously." What? Like I wasn't?)

While the book itself never went to print, I was able to farm out the material and they ended up being published in a number of "Q" anthologies (*Queeries, Quickies* (1 and 2), *Queer View Mirror*), a story, "Puppy Love," that ended up in *The Best Gay Erotica of 1999*, and work that was subsequently featured in *STEAM Magazine*'s first annual Porn Press Awards in a volume called *Stallions & Other Studs*, published by sweet spunky porn star crush Scott O'Hara.

The scuttled book's opening "Invocation" became one of my signature poems, "A Cocksucker's Prayer," along with the stories "God," and "Drunk on Cock," which were selected by none other then an icon of mine at the time, Patrick Califia (famed for their now classic *Macho Sluts*).

This in turn allowed me to attend/read at the OUTwrite Festival in Boston where I met Scott, William J. Mann, and J. Eigo, and led to later readings at Brown University, Universities of Pittsburgh, Toronto, Guelph, the "Bathhouse Series," several AIDS benefits, an appearance on TVO's Imprint on "Writers Who Write About Sex" with Nicholson Baker, Susan Swan, and an editor from Harlequin Romance, as well as the release of three self-published chapbooks: *Cock & Soul* (1991), *The World Is Fucked and Sometimes Beautiful* (1995), and *Bob's Boy* (1996).

A funny story about Imprint (besides my adoration of Daniel Richler's nose at the time)... I read a section of my performance monologue "Bob Smith Sucks Cock," which was met with laughter (and delight?). Later that year I was vacationing at that northern dyke potland called Bancroft and a young lad looked at me and said, "You're that guy!, the guy that read that sex poem on TV!" He later canoed me out on the lake with a garbage bag of weed. A good day.

Then suddenly, the volume of loss of dear friends and relations during the epidemic caught up with me… I hit a wall, hard, was numb and stopped writing.

Full stop.

*

"There's interest of a reissue *Cock & Soul* with the inclusion of two performance works that haven't been published yet."

"Kirby, I want to read new stuff by you." Don Pyle. Telling me what I need to hear. Always.

So, I sat down to it. Attended Sunday's at Hoa Nguyen's poetry class (just enough structure to make me accountable).

I released *She's Having a Doris Day* (KFB, 2017).

O, yes. She opened a poetry bookshop (and press), Knife | Fork | Book (KFB), no longer a brick and mortar (such loss), but occasional pop-ups, a yearly festival (Fertile), and celebrating a tenth anniversary as a publisher as of this writing.

It was at KFB I met some of the most significant people in my life (and they met me in kind).

In many ways, a paradise.

To my good fortune, poet and screenwriter Kathryn Mockler walked into the shop one day.

Me, the ever-excitable fangirl (*squee!*), knowing (and loving) their collection *Onion Man* from Tightrope Books, where I used to work.

The Mockler was incredulous I even knew it/her, let alone featured it on display at the shop.

Poets love to be read. Acknowledged. Who doesn't?

At the time she was running a very popular lit mag, *The Rusty Touque*, and asked if I had anything to send her way.

I sent her three poems from my working manuscript of *This Is Where I Get Off* thinking no one will ever go near this material.

"Kirby, I really like this. Do you have more?"

Which led to, "Kirby, who's editing your book?"

Which led to Matt Finner, who I also met at KFB, still in Kensington, but now located at the The Dark Side Studio (which was dedicated to a belly dance troupe led by the brilliant Audra Simmons when I wasn't selling books).

What can I say?

I was so completely taken with Finner.

Because we were in a dance studio, patrons had to remove their shoes upon entrance, and Matt was wearing white tube socks that said something like "Fuck Off & Die." I was smit.

Little did I know I was meeting the publisher of my debut collection.

Finner was running a burgeoning press, Permanent Sleep, with an edgy punk/hardcore roster (Chris Colohan, Dan Darrah) and distribution through

Deathwish. He was keen on my work. We met, talked, he said yes.

"Let's do this."

It was a dream to work with both The Mockler and Finner. Kathryn kept saying, "Kirby, why do you want to take that out? It's good." God love her "seeing book," when I could only see pieces.

And Matt, agreeing to the cover. A darkly lit corner of urinals with no text. The perfect setting.

We launched *This Is Where I Get Off* at what I can honestly say was one of the most raucous nights of poetry I ever attended/performed at (editor's note: Kirby isn't lying), complete with dancers, projected porn images, an overture, and soundtrack.

If she did nothing else. This night.

But, that's hardly the end of the story.

It was through Finner that I met Stevie Manning. And Bee Traverse.

By the way, first heard of Finner through our mutual friend Don Pyle. They worked/cut hair together (with Stevie) at Town Barber.

Yes, darlins. This is how it works.

As Fairy would say, "This way >>>".

It was Finner who recommended that Stevie get in touch with me to work with them on a collection they wanted to release.

Stevie. Who had a copy of *Poetry is Queer* displayed at their hair station beside CA Conrad and Frank O'Hara.

We met every other week to read through work together. I'd fix us lunch, usually a soup 'n sandwich, or we'd step out to Fran's or Chew Chews…

The resulting KFB chapbook, *Joan Would Say*, was a finalist for the 2024 bpNichol Chapbook Award, and led to Finner putting out Stevie's full-length debut, *Shampoo Boy*, on his new Midnight Mass imprint.

As important as the ground itself, our abiding collegial friendships.

Stevie calls, "Kirby, would you open for me at my launch?"

"Of course, baby. I'm there."

"Is it okay if Derek McCormack joins us?"

"Love me some Derek."

"And Eileen Myles?"

Full stop.

Love how this bitch sets me up.

Who could dream of such a night?

Stevie and Finner, that's who.

What a grand, glorious affair at Standard Time, on the newish "hipster" Geary Avenue strip, packed to the gills… so many faces I haven't seen in forever, and young fresh ones too.

To be invited. Such an honour and a gift.

I wrote to Matt, thanking him saying, "You do realize we're all here (in this configuration) because of you."

And he said, "Kirby, I think we all did this together."

But, that's still not the end of this story.

That handsomely tattooed number standing there off to the side at Standard Time in the Black Sabbath tee…

My beloved friend, poet Jim Johnstone. We also met at KFB, notably carrying Jim's work, as well as the fresh chapbook titles released from Anstruther Press, which he runs with his wife Erica Smith.

Jim lived/shaped the Canadian poetry landscape in significant ways long before I entered the picture. Their own *Misunderstandings Magazine* and editorial work at Palimpsest Press. He's the hardest working person in Poetryland. And faithful. And giving.

And a damn fine poet.

"The Man Who Walks With Me." My favourite descriptor of our friendship. We reflect each other so (dare I say) naturally? Brightly? It is utmost care with the greatest amount of ease.

That great "Air" song refrain, sung by Beth Hirsch:

> You make it easy to watch the world with love
> You make it easy to let the past be done
> You make it easy

I somehow discovered early on, being an earthbound MF Taurus, that I can soar, bust a high-beam, all knowing who I'm entrusting with the kite string. Someone to return my smile and tears.

Beyond success and failure. "I think you're the bee's knees." A friend in poetry.

Rare. And that's what you want. People/artists in your life where/when it is so effortless to be you, and they them, you don't even have to think about it.

And honest, not in any squeaky clean sense, god forbid, and praiseworthy and forgiving on a human scale.

A human scale. Also rare these days.

Someone once said, I was one of those who had this unique capacity to make you feel like you're the only person in the room when I'm with them.

There might be another name for this, but we used to call it *present.*

Not always the easiest of things for anyone, let alone a fairy in the light of day.

Fairy recognizes, responds in kind, to openness.

So, as I was thinking just how Jim and I met, it had something to do with that.

Not transactional. Simply wants for each other to meet/exceed their wants/dreams.

He wasn't afraid me (or I him). This is o so significant.

On a walk, we stop, rest a minute.

"You good?," his hand gently placed on my shoulder, my back.

"Yeah, baby. Thanks."

Jim knows.

We became each other's cheerleaders, me the pretty one with the pom-poms, him, the reason there are Adidas trackies.

One of his [in]famous tee's: MAKE BIG MONEY WRITING POEMS.

Our combined refrain, a saying of Jim's, "Let's do it for the poets."

There are so many Jim stories. We'd hang in the back salon space at KFB camped out on the divans reading poetry to each other, napping, or just chewing the chaw.

He invited me to Fredericton for the legendary Poetry Weekend at the University of New Brunswick hosted by equally legendary Ross Leckie.

This journey east was eye-opening for many reasons, but mostly for how richly people treat each other outside of Toronto. Fact. While I've never been "Toronto-centric," it took getting out of the city to experience welcoming communities that enlarged the picture of myself/KFB in ways I never could've imagined or known.

It can take me quite a while to trust that someone actually might want to be with me. Not, "just being nice," or "wanting something" (they often come as a pair. Imagine).

(If our first meeting is an "ask"... that's not going to bode well.)

On a glorious sunny fall colour-day in Fredericton, Jim invited me to lunch between Poetry Weekend reading sets, and we found a lil' Thai joint just off campus.

The walk there and back from Memorial Hall was as resplendent a picturesque moment a fairy could conjure. We stopped for a selfie.

Then approaching the rather steep hill upon return, my impatient Taurus fear kicked in and I thought to myself, "it's going to take me forever to make it up this hill."

"We got this Kirby. Let's just take our time."

Taking Jim's arm. We made it.

(Does that answer your question?)

Are All Booksellers Dreamers?

It's been donkey's years since I shopped for myself, let alone traveled over an hour to a town I've never visited to set foot in a bookstore I've only heard about. Fuck yes she's excited!

It's a picture perfect day, light traffic on the QEW/403, my friend Katya Nosko at the wheel. Did I ever mention it's a sweet thing to be a passenger? I used to drive living in Ohio, hell everywhere. Walk? Hunny, people would circle for hours in a mall parking lot *not to walk*, curse anyplace sans drive-thru. This was (is) America.

Landing in Toronto was the start of my walking life, cycling younger days, hitting all my book and record shops weekly (12" singles came out Tuesdays). There was the Record Peddler, Driftwood (w/ Don), Sam's, Vortex (w/ Bert), later Rotate/HMV, This Ain't the Rosedale Library, Glad Day (upstairs on Yonge), Pages, Edwards, David Mirvish, Book City (on Bloor), Balfour (across from the Royal), the World's Biggest Bookstore, the shops along Harbord, Ten Editions, Willow, Elliot's (who bought my old gay porn mags before I'd go to the Coach House for the breakfast special or Brother's for chicken pot pie, or a turkey slice across Yonge). A familiar, well trod track.

I still recall with glee scoring the 12" UK import of The Smiths' *Big Mouth Strikes Again* the day it came out, waiting in line at Sam's for the midnight release of Madonna's *Like a Prayer* on vinyl, Mirvish Village on Sundays, blackened chicken livers at Southern Accent, how much Pages felt like a real bookstore, and how cruisy the porn section (actually, the whole) of Glad Day was, making it the BEST pick-up place (not in any way resembling the sterile/correct space it is today).

"Are we going the right way?," Katya, who is a bookseller, owner of The Great Escape Book Store, asks on the drive.

"I think so, it says we're there in three minutes!"

And, viola! Our destination with a parking spot right in front of The (legendary) Printed Word on King Street West (which looks so much like Toronto's Queen Street West 40 years ago) in Dundas, Ontario.

Even before entering, I am enthralled.

What joy is this?

Any brick-and-mortar bookstore that physically features poetry as its oak is an honest to god real bookstore.

I have entered The Printed Word.

We're talking an entire front shop wall of poetry, divided into sections for UK, US, and Canadian poets, with a display of poetic ephemera, a case of rarities and a display rack of chapbooks, with top bins carrying the same.

She is agog. And then there's the books themselves.

She spies/opens the freestanding case of ephemera, which features Brian Dedora's *HUGE*, something I've only heard about.

James says, "I have another Dedora piece that's equally obscure."

Have I fucking died and gone to heaven? Why does this feel so familiar?

This is as Knife | Fork | Book as Knife | Fork | Book ever was.

And bookseller James McDonald is its keeper. The one who is doing everything right.

He's as knowledgeable as he is lovely.

Did I mention he's knowledgeable?

James is a bookseller who knows exactly what he has. With a photographic memory, fluency in spines (of course the books are "in order," his brilliant mind connecting the dots), he's equally conversant with customers combing the philosophy section as he is with a woman who inquires about a poet who recently died.

James lives and breathes The Printed Word. He's a major player to the life of his street, his town, this province, this country. Having met him only to-day, sharing a coffee out front on the sidewalk of Dundas's main drag, I can no longer imagine my world without him.

God how I wish we would've met sooner, maybe struck up some form of collaboration/exchange be-tween our bookshops. Still, James fronts our chap-books so lovingly. Thanks for carrying, tending such a grand vision. A place for lovers, where fingers and eyes meet page.

Floundering (Not Dead)

"People have been tellin' me the Toronto Lit Scene is dead."

About two dozen of us make it out to a poet's book launch in the Junction. A good showing. For many in Toronto, the Junction is viewed as too remote, when there's actually a fairly direct route just off the subway line, with swift express buses from both Dundas West and Keele stations.

But, much like the city itself (off the skids), transit hasn't been altogether pleasant, let alone safe in recent years. I can't last recall when service has been timely, or uninterrupted, without altercation. Tired stretched passengers, just trying to get to where they're going, eyes closed/buds on, people sheltering, fights erupting, tall boy cans, meth smoked openly on platforms.

The day a person rushed onto the streetcar trying to escape their pursuers, blood gushing from their skull onto everyone who couldn't exit fast enough, was the day I decided to close down Knife | Fork | Book's East and West locations.

Toronto's always been… cold. Primarily an SM (Stand and Model) scene. Looking for (but not) the party for a long time now.

They used to be called readings. There used to be exhibits. Interactive simply meant there was a live audience, those in attendance. You thought nothing of going to places of interest.

Now, there's designated spots to take Instagram photos. An exhibition? A reading? It's either a "must," a "to be seen" (or streamed) event, or it's not on Google Maps.

I'm hard pressed to think of a single place I have a desire to go. Sure: New York, Berlin, the East Coast, Iceland. A girl can dream. But not in Toronto.

The problem isn't depression, though it appears so at times. It's closer to poverty. Depletion. Loss. More associated with loss of familiarity, of character. A lack of presence. Days have ceased to accumulate. Each day is simply something to manage. Get thru. Hope you didn't forget anything.

Is it real if it doesn't scroll?

On Sunday I go to the opening of the Brian Dedora/ Michael Dean Contact Photography show at The

Secret Handshake on College. Almost gave up on the streetcar, which was a 30 minute wait both ways in the rain, but the show was great and I got to sit with the artists and meet a few new folks, be present in real life.

Made my way down Augusta in Kensington Market where Knife | Fork | Book used to be (so much of my life, this street) to hang with my besties, Joseph and Leo at Orbital Arts Gallery. They've been together for 30 years now. I'm always amazed they can still make a go (in business). I guess, like me, the answer lies in the making and making do.

We plant seeds for a new joint project, share a sip of single malt. Toast to my own belated on C.P. Cavafy's birthday (also the day of his death at 70). I didn't know we were but a week apart. Smoky. Peaty. Perfect.

Thank god for distractions. They insist. Bring/keep me present.

I take a break to fold laundry. Fresh T-shirts! (not off the clothesline, but...). I used the last of the dryer sheets Suzanne gave me ("who's going to look after Kirby when I'm gone?").

"What's wrong? You can tell me. Do you need anything?"

As master printer Andrew Steeves asked on my pilgrimage to Gaspereau Press earlier this month (our meeting, such good fortune), “Have you had a meal today?”

Tuna w/capers and red onion on a brioche bun. Fancy.

Such passion, creators/artists who make things with their hands, with what they have, daily. Eek out a living.

It’s pains me to see so many struggle. That’s what it is. There’s little room for ease these days.

All energies to incur an income to try to make ends meet. Trying to make something matter when the whole world seems at best on hold.

My gay bestie texts: “We could be in Palm Springs blowing pensioners for doubles CHER!!!”

Fuck, how many times must they test the fire alarm at my residence?

Gay Bestie: “With witty banter like…‘GIRL your shirt’s on backwards and you smell like balls.’”

Sweet baby jesus thank the gods I’m gay.

"I'm feeling so invisible," a poet shares, and I'm surprised, because they're not invisible to me. I'm seated right here.

"I don't feel a part of [name a community you think exists]."

"O, darlin' bless your heart, there is no poetry community. Nip that one right in the bud." We laugh.

"There are poets, mostly pleasantly unto themselves, some wondering if anybody notices, or reads them, or gives a fuck either way. The gossips, those who they agree with, tear people down. Or they may belong to a writer's group (a context, not a community), or they've cultivated a circle of select friends over the years. Cherished relationships you share your work with, or not."

"Women tend to show up for each other. Various peoples with a shared common interest. A few intimates/confidants, rare. Those you play with, also rare. The good fortune of likes crossing differences."

Who hasn't thought, "What if nobody shows up?" It happens.

Like you, I'm tired. Days shouldn't be this hard and it sucks when everything is so costly, especially if you have holes in your pockets. When, like many including myself, you live in (financial) poverty, which compounds into daily uncertainties.

But once poverty reaches the imagination, there's a K-hole. Game stopper.

Clean those plugs darlin'. Time to rest, reimagine. Open a window, if not a door.

Never forget, it's all about good lighting (not a phone charger). I can't read Henri Cole's sonnets off the page without a decent lamp.

My freezer is full. I haven't lost my apartment. Made the sandwich Suzanne used to fix for me.

Time for my walk. She gets out when she can. Even when she's broke/n. Not entirely up for it.

And she's writing. And reading you. And my badass sister CAConrad arrives this weekend.

And darlins, we're the party. The shift. Let's not just sit around bitchin' and complaining that things suck here. Everybody already knows how much. Let's make change, transform beyond all recognition.

Liberation

"Slobber all you want."

How To Support Yourself As An Artist

Anne Michaels: "Kirby, how can you afford to do all this?"

Me: "She's used to flying by the seat of her pants."

*

Today, I have a total of $319.01 in my bank account (fifteen days shy of my next deposit).

No credit. No sock drawer. I live primarily on my pension/seniors income of approximately $1800/month.

In Toronto.

And I live well.

I have held many jobs this lifetime. Most of them "volunteer," as in either little to no monetary income, never a salary, or benefits.

Which has placed me pretty much at or below what's called the "poverty line" much my adult life.

I have no idea how money works. Like my father's business (sheet metal), you either had money or you didn't, but you always managed, struggled, even when it meant going without on occasion.

"It's only me," my mother when she was on her own would say, "I don't need much."

Luck, baby. Good fortune. And, there's ways you can help it along.

It helps to live simply.

"Have you gotten your name in at a co-op yet?"

Never mind how long the wait list is. You never know what's gonna happen, when your name might pop-up.

And it will, but you gotta be on the list to begin with.

For me, in the 90s, a surprisingly short 18 month wait to receive notice that a bachelor apartment was available at City Park Cooperative in the Village.

Just in time, since where I was living was experiencing an unfortunate rise in crack-use, and the manager was sliced up pretty bad "interrupting a deal" while taking out the trash.

On the flip side, it was mostly bachelor apartments coming up because of how AIDS was ravaging our community. (Again, completely a fluke I was/am still alive.)

I qualified for the brilliant Rent Geared to Income program at City Park. That's a third of my income, monthly. Doable. As an added bonus, co-op members voted to install our own servers (internet/TV) on site, which for a nominal fee (less than $30/month) is included in our rent. I imagine this might also suffice as someone's online phone (looking into it).

I couldn't afford a phone when I first moved out on my own in the Old West End, Toledo, Ohio (mid to late 70s, long before the internet). I used the TARTA bus system to get to work, anywhere. Got food stamps for staples. Like my parents, I learned ways to make ends meet (with the expressed dream of 'saving anything' being only a dream).

You best believe I've performed for my dinner (still do). I'd put up notices around my residence when I first arrived in Toronto for a summer training program, make a few bucks, then head down to the same day vegetable rack at Baldwin's to see what I'd be fixing to eat that night.

Similar to how my mom would take her younger brother popcorn when he was in university so he had something to eat.

I was still awaiting "landed immigrant" status when I first arrived, and of course it was friends of a friend who came to my rescue, offering bouncing jobs at all-night candy stores, goth nights in empty warehouse spaces on Richmond Street, at the Rivoli, and a dyke bar on Bond Street.

This didn't feel like hardship. It was living.

My first "landed" job was as an attendant care worker assisting people with spinal cord injuries so they could live independently. Meals, dressing, bathing, bowel movements. My focus became what it would be like to be on the receiving end of care. Role-reversals have always informed, directed, shaped my empathy.

Yes, I've cried sitting in a welfare office. "You didn't imagine ending up here did you?"—the kind official handed me a box of tissues.

She's fallen through a few cracks. Got the help I needed. Landed. Picked myself back up. (With help/assistance). Found my footing.

Luck. The unbelievable good fortune of having enough good people/friends around me that loved/relished me (even "broke" me) and I them.

With what I have, I'm generous to a fault (they say). The coat off my back.

Hell, like you, like those before us, all trying to make a go of it, another day.

Laughs, a bevy out, dancing.

"You good baby? Here, let me get that. Next time."
kisses

I don't know if things are any harder these days, but I do know they're not any easier… I still have to muster, see to it I'm not on fumes last week of the month.

Once again, my co-op came to the rescue, teamed up with the University Health Network where I now receive a small FoodShare box every other week.

Like a good senior, she read the notice in the mailroom.

Like housing, food is a right.

Let me tell you, when the FoodShare box arrives it's a little like Christmas. I never know just what I'm getting, but I can tell you it's fresher and prettier than what they call produce at the Blaws. Stuff I want to fix a meal with. Feast. Enjoy.

Call me pig in shit. Happy. She loves to cook. She used to love moving lawns for the same reason. Nothing organizes, cleans my clock, clears my clutter more. Serve that goodness up in an orange dish with a spoon.

And to be able to share good eats with my theatre friend upstairs.

I've also lost 3 sacks of potatoes (30+ pounds since April 2026), and my walk, which has pained me the past year or so, has returned to me thanks to compassionate care (CBD) and my Feldenkrais practice. There's a joy in my step.

There's a lovely broadcaster on Jazz FM 91.1 who always closes out her program by saying, "I know your lives are busy, thanks for choosing to spend this time with us, I really appreciate it… and be sure to check in on someone who might be alone or having a go of it these days. Be kind when you can."

Thank you dear reader. To making ends meet (and a little cush). To us.

What I learned from social media

If there's one thing Spoken Word, or Slam Poetry, has given us, it's the current. The now. With cadence and a heartbeat.

Sure, these poets are playing to finger-snapping, enrapt audiences, aiming to 'win'… yes, their art could be 'stand-up,' or 'rap' but…

The word is alive, vibrant, and real.

Poet Britta B dances: "I'm the only black person in this room!" On repeat. At a lit festival in Sudbury. I so wanted to get up, dance with her in joy.

At an award ceremony Britta hosted, she was the warmest being in the room. (Thanks for the shout-out babe, that and coming to my table, loving me).

These things don't go unnoticed. How do we live without?

We are so bereft of basic kindness.

This imaginary all too real gap between industry and artists. Who gets seen. Awarded.

Like you, I rejoice with those who rejoice. Weep with those who weep.

My arms stretch out wide.

To be your mosh pit this night. Lean in. I'm here for it.

People just want an ounce.

CanLit? Stingy Can-fucking-Lit.

A poet I admire says "social media is so embarrassing."

I can't disagree.

Another checks their feed in visible duress: "I usually get more likes by now."

Might as well be Grindr. Plenty-O'-Fish.

"Dick pic?" [exit left].

An early Felice Picano poem, "Slashed to Ribbons in Defense of Love," vying for likes, a repost.

Something tangible. Like passing a joint… a bump, caress.

See me. Like me. Follow me.

Back to my cubicle at the baths.

My reading room for the hour.

Read to me. The timbre of your voice, the downcast softness of your eyes.

Read to me. My most recognizable, immediate familiar.

That, and a beat.

There's nothing sexier than being read to by a stud in a towel. Taking in the faint sweetness of exhales. Spooning.

How I Loved Your Love

One recent morning I wakened to this in my message box from a dear friend:

About James Baldwin, Toni Morrison said, "Your tenderness—a tenderness so delicate I thought it could not last, but last it did and envelop me it did… You knew, didn't you, how I loved your love? You knew."

Now I do.

> "The longer I live, the more deeply I learn that love—whether we call it friendship or family or romance—is the work of mirroring and magnifying each other's light."
>
> —James Baldwin,
> *Nothing Personal*

There is but one struggle: the struggle to be here, damaged and all. "There is no hierarchy to oppression," said Audre Lorde. It's a courageous act to continue.

And this is nearly impossible without "accurate reflectors." Trusted intimates, perhaps a stranger whose naked radiant face is truly open.

"Magnifying each other's light."

I also refer to such people as "touchstones," those who have the ability to immediately connect us to/ remind us of a self we misplace at times that in this reflective light, brings us to the here and now. Our exquisite selves. My Fairy.

"I see you."

Branding/marketing, AI will have none of it. What we see is a fabrication of what something is supposed to be, look like, sound like, but strangely not feel like. An idea of the dream. Not the dream itself.

Your dream.

I only recently came across Chappell Roan's *Pink Pony Club* online—not her official video (which is a hoot) but the positively infectious viral lip-synching video by TrinoxAdam on TikTok (@trinoxadam). Goodness, the rapturous love these two share.

And the joy of a good pop song.

As Langston Hughes quickens: "We / Who have nothing to lose / Must sing and dance."

Why wait? There's "Nothing Left To Lose" (Everything But The Girl), much of this summer (the year, ffs), "poof" gone, or as my dance buddy Christopher says, "Lay it all down babe." And I do, dancing my tits off to RuPaul's "The Realness," around 6pm daily.

Oppressed peoples have always found ways to dance in the face of adversity, often as an act of defiance, a means of survival, the express purpose of ecstasy, joy. Anthems help us rise up.

If anyone was to tell me in 2024 that I'd be enraptured in my living room movin' and groovin' to new Pet Shop Boys (one of their best albums EV-VAH, the gift of a lifetime), I wouldn't have believed them. Check these opening Neil Tenant lines from the first single, "Loneliness":

> There is a better fight
> A cause close to my heart
> The struggle against loneliness
> That's tearing you apart

Lush strings and orchestrations swell to one of the most recognizable beats/sounds in queer music history—that and a video to pine over. Who else but the PSB to make your lonely-ass get up and dance?!

Maybe it's not your cuppa, but it's worth finding out what your lifelines, your reflectors, your touchstones are. What moves, keep you here.

"Best advice I ever got was an old friend of mine, a black friend, who said you have to go the way your blood beats. If you don't live the only life you have, you won't live some other life, you won't live any life at all. That's the only advice you can give anybody. And it's not advice, it's an observation."

James Baldwin, at 100, on high beam.

Spill the T

"Today, I genuinely feel like a bride of Poetry. Several times, I left men who intruded upon my Poetry and writing because no man has ever been my primary relationship."

—CAConrad

Our beloved friend and "bride of Poetry," CAConrad, is celebrating their 50th year wedded to the craft.

This is where/how it all began: some 15 years ago upstairs at the Imperial Pub I attended a CA workshop that re-lit my pilot light after years of devastating loss during the AIDS crisis. It's where Hoa Nguyen (and subsequently Dale Smith) and I met, before I joined Hoa's Sunday afternoons reading and writing through Frank O'Hara.

I hadn't read a word by any of them prior to CA's workshop, but knew I wanted to write again, and hoped this might be a kick-start. It was that and more: a clearing. Fresh air. Lifting pencil to poetry. Lifting myself.

CA judged the 2025 Queer Poetry Prize at Palette Poetry, "Celebrating Queer Poetry in the New Age of Heterosexual Violence and Absolute Stupidity!"

In an interview they were asked, "What are some of your favourite examples of queer poetry?" and right off the top they replied:

"A remarkable book from last year that is anti-corporate, anti-national, pro-queer body, and pro-queer sex is called *She* by my dear friend Kirby from Knife | Fork | Book. Kirby also lost many friends in the early years of the AIDS crisis, and you can feel the 'I'm not taking shit from anybody' vibe all over their pages!"

From the OG of the "I'm not taking shit from anybody vibe," this is the highest praise! Happy 50th sweet sis!

I recently received a card (in the mail!) from fellow poet Susan Wismer, with an essential quote from the great Jeanette Winterson:

"She must find a boat and sail in it. No guarantee of shore. Only a conviction that what she wanted could exist, if she dares to find it."

Included inside: "One small note of kindness… to say thank you, thank you for your presence, your honesty, your truth—there's far too little of you in this world."

At the same time, this overwhelming letter (of recommendation) received "out of the blue" from poet, Luke Hathaway:

"As trans and nonbinary voices are silenced, erased from the record, and/or suppressed (daily tidings of this just now from the States), I think about wanting to lift up the voice of a transplanted queer American-Canadian who has spent a lifetime making space for queer and trans and gender-nonconforming voices: Kirby, of Toronto. As the force behind the beloved Kensington Market all-poetry bookstore Knife | Fork | Book (est. 2016 and continuing in spirit—and as a small-press publishing house—beyond the demise of its Kensington Market location); as the author of my personal bible *Poetry is Queer*; as the director of the Fertile Festival of New and Inventive Works; and in I suspect many other capacities, Kirby has invited all of us to lift up and celebrate our inner (or not so inner!) queerness, to enter into community with one another, to respect our differences, to celebrate our sexuality/ies and asexualities without shame. A liberatory voice and a force for good. We need Kirby now more than ever.

A personal anecdote:

When I transitioned, at the age of 41, in the midst of a literary career—and came out as a trans, queer and nonbinary man—Kirby was one of the first to embrace me, saying simply, 'I've always got room in my heart for a new pocket of queerness.' Bless them.

They are the queer parent I never had. They hold space not just for queerness but for poetry. They remind us that poetry is queer!—a liberatory space of language use which, for all our sakes, we must continue to make and to rejoice in."

I share this not out of any self-aggrandizement, but because I had no idea. We so rarely hear who we are to others. I responded to Luke saying as much:

"Isn't it funny how we simply meet/read each other in kind relishing/drinking in the moment, only then to realize later HOW EXTRAORDINARY that it was/is possible at all in these dark days."

Luke, what an honour and privilege to be Kirby in your life.

To be. To be with each other. To lift each other up, hold each other dear.

This is who we are (or can be). Lifelines. Anchors. Wells to drink from. Where the language of poetry and other poets nourishes, sustains, revives, and urges our radiant [queer] selves.

To find footing we didn't realize we had, often in the nick of time.

I would not be Kirby without CA, or Hoa, or Dale, or Susan, or Luke, or Jim, or The Mockler, or countless others, even those I may never realize are connected to me through writings, presence, being.

To list each of you whose faces are my immediate, the entirety of who I am.

Or as sister Sandra Bernhard knew all too well, *Without You I'm Nothing.*

As I'm writing this it happens to be International Transgender Day of Visibility. It's nice to have a day. Better still to walk down the street without fear or threat of violence.

Much is made of the "joy " in my work. That's my Fairy, the one (thank the homocats) I never managed to kill. But know, my queen is pissed and on guard, at the ready.

The joy of being Kirby is that I see you everyday.

Goodbyes

Though the companionship is dearly missed, I can't have another cat. Another loss.

Goodbyes slay me.

That moment the Windsor train departs for Toronto, Suzanne on the platform makes all the signs telling me not to cry.

I hate leaving her.

How many more trips/times to embrace, wave goodbye?

Like that brilliant scene in Amy Tan's *The Joy Luck Club,* where the mother mouths, "I see you! I see you!"

I see you. A mother's calling.

During the AIDS epidemic, I had to stop going (to memorials). I know they're held for the people who show up, and yes, that can matter, but "He was a light," on repeat, grew beyond my capacity.

I already know what memorials, death look like.

I wanted all of them to live.

Throw on a track and dance to me. Deal?

Suzanne wanted what Wally had: viewing, open casket, flowers, the same funeral home, the works.

Girl. You know she can't be in the same room as a dead body.

No, she doesn't "look good." She is not here. I don't know that corpse. Thank you.

My friend David died while catching glimpses of online boys in a frat house going about their business, a spilled bottle of poppers by his side.

Well done, darlin'.

Yes, I should've attended yours. I wanted to. Planned to. Failed.

Jim's. Such a good man. A caring friend. He deserved my presence there.

At Eleanor's (Suzanne's mother, my heart) I lost it. Threw myself bawling on her corpse in the box. They had to pull me off and carry me out.

Like praise, there's no half-measure to grief.

She can't simply go through the motions.

Besides, these loved ones have never left me, they walk with me. Every step.

Everywhere I look, Suzanne sees what I see.

We pause. That breeze. See her face in mine taking it all in.

The very same face I see stepping off the train, rushing to greet me as she always has.

Daily.

Do Your Homework

I used to think that people didn't like being told what to do. And, while there may be choice exceptions, ("On your knees, boy"), truth is most of us want to be told what to think, what to believe, what to wear, what to eat, see, read, and especially what to do to get it right (keep a job/have a life). We even seek it out, pay for it (at times, dearly).

All very human of us. We do indeed learn from, copy one another. Create new familiars.

Nowhere is this more magnified or played out more exhaustively than the algorithms of social media platforms, our new communal "pornograph": food porn, fashion porn, book porn, emoji porn, Brooklyn apartment porn, animal rescue porn, music porn, shopping porn, protest porn, buy this, eat here, brand brand brand fuck the system scroll scroll scroll link in bio.

Some might mistake this for community. At best, it may simply inform my calendar ("Oooooooo! I didn't know this was happening!," hopefully it hasn't passed already as is often the case.)

At worst? One interchangeably bland branding publicist/influencer after another. Today's spin and spiel. "Nothing to see here. Move along."

Now, before you go ballistic on me ("ballistic" gleefully reimagined in this moment) you're speaking to someone who has as much lived experience pre-internet as with. I'm with Douglas Coupland, who posits, "I Miss My Pre-Internet Brain."

One had to go to such marvellous lengths to keep abreast of what was happening back in the day. I'd have to step out to the corner, pick up a newspaper, a copy of *After Dark, Dance Magazine, Christopher Street, The Body Politic*, walk the neighbourhood, happen upon a flier (either rip it off for my bedroom, or note the date/place), all a creative map of discovery, a personal way of connecting the dots, points of reference, knowing things. Mapping a life.

Not to mention the limitless possibilities of like others, and chance meetings.

A better life? No, just different. What, for me anyway, was a human scale. Expectant. Curious. Encounters. Adventures. Daily.

"She's never wanted to be anything other than flesh and blood this lifetime"—*Poetry is Queer.*

Not a chip. Not an implant. She still insists on the physical book in hand so that her eyes remain practiced, don't lose their ability to focus/read across a page (fighting their urge to scroll).

So funny, the first books: tablets/scrolls.

Don't get me wrong. Like you, I love, use it all. She just prefers paper. Easier on the eyes, brain.

But, in significant ways, life on the internet pales in comparison. Is it just me/my age, or does it strike any of you as less human? It has taken up considerable real estate in how we engage mentally, physically.

My measure has always been, and continues to be, "Is there any life in it?"

I will simply say this. The one thing that hasn't changed for me is that all of my memories, the times I remember, recall, dream... none of these are of time online. Not one.

Have you noticed? Is it the same for you?

(There was this time decades ago I had to stop playing Tetris when falling blocks from the sky began to invade my dreams... idk, does that count?)

So, here's your homework.

Queer icon/artist John Cameron Mitchell posted this great quote while putting on their make-up:

"Your homework is to stop cancelling each other, find out about punk, and get laid while you're at it."

Charming John Fucking Cameron Mitchell. Two of the most outrageously queer creations I've ever seen were *Hedwig and The Angry Inch*, and their raucously extraordinary sexcapade of a film in search of an orgasm *Shortbus* (essential queer viewing). They just got off their Broadway run as the lead in *Oh, Mary!* to embark on a 25th anniversary movie tour of Hedwig. (She bows.)

I believe the homework is self-explanatory and doesn't require anything further from me. A gift from John. On Instagram.

sprite

Kiss

Across the rainbow
crosswalk off
my balcony stands

yet another fronted
by large block letters—
"Love Makes a Family."

Two bearded furry men
in harnesses deep
tongue one another

while stroller dad
baby in one arm
takes a slew of shots

to post on their feed.
Before even a wisp
of Pride gay boys

staged a kiss-in
at Yonge & Bloor
and were arrested—

public indecency—
fined for their lip-
locks. Convicts.

Made the papers.
"You were supposed
to feel ashamed

of yourselves." Some
want to keep us
from their children—

"They're too young."
Formative. Didn't keep
me from imagining

certain shapes, forms
"We two boys
together Clinging."

A Toronto film critic refused
to review queer films
so revulsed by "the kiss."

At the Union Station
photo booth, curtain shut,
my boyfriend & I kiss.

He's seeing me off—
Orchestral Manoeuvres in the Dark
"So In Love"—

when a shadow appears,
officer in black shoes
accosts us—"I don't care

what you do in your own
homes but in public
it's an offence"

as though anyone could see
us through the dark
fabric two guys in a cubicle

our love our lives
suspect criminal.
I board the train

no hug goodbye only tears,
a wave, that filmstrip
our wedding invite not yet legal,

but Unitarians
will marry anyone.
Kiss my darlings.

I am so proud of you.
Never mistake
pride for liberation.

Kiss them all.

At Long Last Love

"I'm homosexual... How and why are idle questions. It's like wanting to know why my eyes are green."

—Jean Genet

Genet, you and I have always known this. It's been a given my entire queer life. The ground I walk on.

And, she can walk.

After 6 months my walk has returned to me. Fluid. No clunks. Without effort or having to think about it.

And, not to brag, but this lil' old fairy can put on their socks and wipe their butt too.

Clipping my own toenails is getting easier.

Clever, ain't she? (Fairy nods. Giggles.)

This has been where Fairy has always lead me... "what would be easier, baby?"

Easier. Less needless effort.

Good lube? Essential.

Like its predecessor/s, *Poetry is Queer* (and *She*), meeting/writing *Fairy* has forever changed me.

Why else write a book?

With *PIQ*, I set out to create a constellation/map of queer poet guides that became my familiars, held me dear, continue to keep me here. With *She* I simply wanted to refine my poetics, hone my use of language during a second wave of great loss in my life.

But loss is a tricky thing. Often sudden, harsh, with survival in question. You may move through it, or this may be it. The stopper.

Indecision has never served me. Not even once.

There are two sandbars/traps for me: the place of indecision, and the place of no longer caring.

The Land of Not Pretty.

Fairy knows. "Enter at your own risk."

One could teeter, be tempted to linger… dip, peek only to be swallowed whole.

I think this is why even the idea of (solitary) confinement, crawlspaces, any place where I cannot stand/breathe/move about freely terrifies.

I don't go places I cannot leave of my own free will.

I'm not afraid of the dark—I can move, even sit with you in the dark.

Hell, I'll even fall, or drown.

It's being buried alive that I can't handle. (I nearly had to leave *Kill Bill Vol.2*. Uma! Buried! In a box! With a light!).

Fairy thrives in open spaces.

She doesn't require a lot of space. Just enough to move, breathe.

Freely.

To be trapped. Absconded. Bag over your head. Handcuffed. Jailed. Tortured. Abused. Hung.

To gasp for breath.

These are daily realities to contend with. Mentally. Physically.

One my Fairy continues to imagine, invent some creative play around.

A trusted partner knows the sign, holds me at first struggle.

Holds. Pulls out.

Gasp. Slobber. Glory.

"Open." Again. Tap. Release.

Air.

Love me a good trusty pipe cleaner.

My Fairy's relationship to the deities.

Ecstasies at play. Not authorities.

To freely worship, embrace what you love.

The beauties I encounter/converse with everywhere I look.

I am vibratory with the foods I select—they call out, speak to me like the blooms on my walks, wave "Hello lovelies!"

Prepare, feast upon plant, repot, soil.

So much of what we know as life is hell-bent to conform, consume, be liked, belong.

When belonging only requires being here. And, I am. That's the given. The elusive obvious.

Trying to be here, while at times called upon (even daily), is my default, not my practice.

To hear things as an invite. A request. Not a demand.

It's not even based on what one might like to do. There are menial tasks… I suppose.

But, even those, there's life to be found in them.

“Where's the life in this?”

Fairy: “This way>>>”.

Some call it a trick, or a game. Sure! That's the play.

There's things I don't want to do, that I'm made to or have to do. To live, makes ends meet.

Those are “the ends.” My joy is in the discoveries of how we do so in all varieties.

Some, kin to my skin. Others? I also marvel.

It's the how that's kaleidoscopic, continues to fascinate, keeps me fresh, curious… imaginative. Makes wonder.

I'm not a positive person, nor optimistic. To "better" myself isn't a strong or even a primary motivator.

There's goodness here that works, is already at play.

What's the song of this moment? It awakens my body to sing, laugh, cry.

That's why the direction is always more. More Kirby. More life.

Most of my primary relationships are with "the dead."

Or what we call dead. These relations are not dead to me. I listen, converse, at times learn, but mostly, am attuned to their revelations: yes, this too is human.

Animal, plant, the elements, life and death. Rebirth.

How do you greet the day? Or does it just happen to you?

Of course, the day will likely happen whether I'm present or not. There were days, weeks, years where

I could only be present to a certain square footage… even when it was only the pain that impaired my walk.

Or heaviness, the sadness of being wronged, oppressors out to take any remaining ounce of life.

Don't let them darlins. And don't do that work for them.

I don't have to make them right, or right them, or conform to their idea of "right."

Life is not a test to pass. "Can I make it through?" "Why can't I be like other people?" "If only I could…"

Something is afoot, is obviously working, or at play, because you're here, with me, reading these words.

Yes, there are obstacles, real or imagined. Powers at play often condition us to be what others want, erect hoops to jump through, laws against us (our bodies, our very existence).

That's why there must be basic rights. The autonomy of our bodies. Housing. Food. Health care. Chosen work. Whom we choose to love.

People continue to move/migrate all over this earth in search of what is livable. (Sadly, these days, not sustainably like most of human history).

Mere existence?

Oppressive powers rarely share the wealth of our beings. Poverty exists in this absence.

Oppressors—have you seen the lives they live? The ones who will destroy before someone "other" can live.

This is not my life. But, it is the current I swim in.

Fairy knows. Tosses me a line.

Beware the undertow. The K-holes. Weapons of mass incarceration. Destruction.

There is no life there.

Evenings, I head to YouTube.

Watch Miguel show me the foods he found from the waters, land to sup today. What makes him smile and makes him strong. Such pleasure to share a meal with him.

Follow shipmates who rescue my beloved sea creatures (like Cecil the Seasick Sea Serpent), clean/clear the barnacles off tortoises and whales, bathe them and return them new to the waters.

Or wolves, deer, foxes, owls, all of my favourite animals who seek help, assist a loved one somehow trapped, or their child injured, not able to move from the mud, free themselves from a wire fence or plastics or a damaged wing, at times lost/abandoned.

Led to by a loved one. A mate. Out to seek help. Found. Retrieved. Repaired. Nursed. Tended to back to life. Set free.

Often, to return with a gift of thanks. (A sea cucumber. To play in the yard with their young.)

People dancing in the faces of their oppressors. Or alone in their rooms. To our gaylord and saviour Bad Bunny.

There is no greater joy than to see the body celebrate.

These are the things that move me, keep me here. Make me bust a chair dance on a Saturday night.

The queers play now, as ever, everywhere, that gay pulse, under threat of death, but no, tonight we live, slay, do the duck walk, prance, shuffle, make out, bodies touching bodies, currents of the night that cause us to swoon, want more.

"Last night a DJ saved my life." "Meeting in the ladies room." "Omg, perfect nipples!"

We know. We are here, we're queer. They haven't destroyed us. Nor will they. My body, yours, is living proof.

Fairy knows. Fairies are free.

Tending to Each Other's Freedom

In Michael Nardone's delightfully readable (and recommended) *Convivialities* (Talonbooks, 2025), he sources "radical educator" Ivan Illich's use of the term:

> Conviviality: an "autonomous and creative intercourse among persons, and the intercourse of persons with their environment," which he considers "to be individual freedom realized in personal interdependence [...] and limit this freedom only in favour of another member's equal freedom [...] in Illich's sense of the word, conviviality is thus a repertoire for attending to the commons of culture, for nuturing its robustness and capacity for difference."

Tending to each other's freedom. Robustly so. Radical to this day.

There are numerous revelatory moments in convivial conversation throughout Nardone's book, written in such a way that as a reader I felt freed in the exact same moment of what was found on the page.

Poets/artists tend in creative intercourse. What engages, delights. That which is ours to do.

I also had the immense gift of attending Compagnie Hervé Koubi's *What the Day Owes to the Night* (Luminato Festival) where Koubi describes a group of Algerian "street dancers":

> Going on the quest of this day to give it strength and form as one goes in search of The Truth or more exactly of a truth [...] a marvellous transposition of my paths and those traversed by each of the dancers encountered in Algeria, as so many threads mingling and intertwining, so many links also unite us in a history and a geography [...] Links to be found, others to be renewed and still others to be built.

You never know when you're going to enter the temple.

What do we owe the night? Pure majesty—in vision, execution, form—thirteen extraordinary dancers interdependent, reliant, radiant, in support of each other's being and their own. Shining brilliance.

Majesty... Paul Taylor's *Airs*, Alvin Ailey's *Revelations,* Bill T. Jones/Arnie Zane Dance Company's *Uncle Tom's Cabin/The Promised Land,* Compagnie Hervé Koubi's *What the Day Owes to the Night.*

O, what our bodies can do!

First night, I sat at "foot level" in row B... I have come to see the gods after all and yes, they're here in abundance, entering/re-entering, skirted men in flight, lifted, thrown, tossed, caught/released, spinning, rotating again and again mid-air, cloths twirling on their heads, arms outstretched to grasp, eyes never leaving their fellow beings in motion, tending to each other in revelry.

I immediately bought a seat in the second row balcony the following evening to witness these energies, glorious bodies, their formations from a different (no less intimate) distance.

What entranced me so? This is High Church, and I but a temple boy, held in the awe of it all, bearing witness, beholding the beauty that burns so fiercely. These men showing that liberation is possible.

Agnes Martin:

> Beauty is the mystery of life. It's not in the eye, it's in the mind. And, it's because of awareness of perfection in the mind. As a matter of fact I think we see perfection and then we see beauty. You know they're different. Like I see a—I look down at a valley and

> think, aw it's just perfect. Perfection is easier to see than beauty. You look at the sky and it's perfect. And then you look further and it's beautiful. You enter into it and all that. Beauty illustrates happiness. The wind in the grass. You know how happy the grass looks. And the shining waves following each other.

The temple. Fairy knows.

Koubi wrote a poem called "I Went There" that was read aloud (in Arabic) closing the piece:

> I went there to the other side of the sea
> which saw me grow up on an unknown land
> that was nevertheless mine.
>
> I went there to see the streets, the houses and the tombs.
>
> I went there without knowing what I was looking for.
>
> I went there to face the emptiness.
>
> I went there to meet my lost brothers.
>
> I went there and my tears flowed at the
> oblivion and the cruel time that had passed.

I went there and brought back to my heart my finally found brothers.

I went there full of brotherly love nowhere else known.

I went there out of love for them and for mine.

I went there because I believe in the power of love and spirit.

I went there.

I went there…

There's a new cashier at Loblaws. Kevin. O. mg. Just. My. Type. (Bearded, tall, South Asian?, slender, stunning.)

"I love your brooch," he smiles.

"It was my mom's," I beam, blush, bib-less, pulling out my favourite handkerchief, an orange paisley number to mask any imaginary drool. She has no poker face when it comes to desire. Never has.

"Is that silk? Where can I find one of those in the city? I've been looking all over."

"I know. They're not easy to come by. I got this in Kensington Market at Courage My Love."

"Courage My Love?" with a quizzical look on his face that endears me to him even more.

Those lips, those eyes. This close.

"Yes, Courage," describing the iconic vintage clothiers that have been open as long as I've lived in Toronto.

"Is your mother still with us?"

“She is today,” I smile (we smile) bagging my half-off goods. Soup fixins.

“Would you like your receipt?” I turn, hands collide, eyes meet. Laughter.

“Keep warm.”

“You as well, my friend.”

The Pink Root

"Perhaps the hardest thing for a woman to learn is
That she was never the problem."

—Adrienne Rich

Mere acceptance?

Don't do me any favours.

It's either a lavender light

or it's a no go—

I want an open window

a door motioning

This way >>>

Not the path of least

resistance, those who

never cared or wanted

me. To live.

Move towards all
that makes you smile
Your belly quake,
your face blast
Each frame stills each
moment a treasure rings
rings of an oak
sister mojo your hand.

A grounding the ground
itself without which
there is no rest.
No sky. No moon.
Blessed assurance. This oak.

Voices carry

Frustrating day not the day

itself picture book perfect

It's my walk that's laboured no

ease pleasure a bit of the Tin Man

not my affectionate Scarecrow

Sissyboy Leonardo still, she makes

her way, cause it matters

cause she wants to hear

the poets near the fire pit

Withrow Park I thought was north

on Logan, thank goddess Leni scooped

me up at Chester Station

"Love your new cut!" baring

a picnic basket of baked

sweet potato bread such love

to walk with me, slow as I am

(patience Taurus)

Not much harms/phases me now

or it all does (What hasn't she

lived through?) We're going to

a city park near the old Bain Co-op,

no ICE, masked nazis just

remnants. New hippies in the breeze

meeting hearing poetry beneath a tree.

This way >>>

Fairy knows when to exit.

Even looked into the "how" (never one to leave a mess).

Always figured she'd stay as long as she's useful

Still enjoy's themself, the view. If there are limbs

forms that quicken my pulse—that wild wisp

of a curl off a forehead. Knowing wink and a smile.

"What's left for this fairy to do?"

A dear poet friend when asked "What's next?," replies,

"I'm DONE. I don't think the world needs another one of my books." How fucking refreshing. To be, to know, fin.

And, decide, make it so. I still find myself picking up sticks.

Like Ennis, sworn beneath my breath to quit for years

only to return to the very stream where we first met,

Fairy and me, one and the same, cross the stone bridge

our private path along the crick to where it bends round

a willow. Perhaps the opposite bank curved like a sk8r's

ramp, the water cascading across pockets, mini waves,

rivulets backlit by sunlight, the appearance of scales

on a shimmering carp. She'd take off all her clothes,

cool my bum seated on the softest patch of bright green

moss, Fairy's throne! And the breeze would make

the willow caress my face and sometimes she'd sing softly

to dragonflies, birds. But, mostly, she just sat there.

I know what I want to do for the rest of my life!

I want to be read to. My beautiful Fairy in the shape
of you

comes, joins me each night, soft cotton tee, socks,

favourite pair of jeans… I re-create a throne of sorts,

pillows to prop your back as you snuggle in,

your hand tapping, beckoning, smoothing the space

between your open legs, a hovel for me to rest my head

on your inner thigh as you read Genet to me:

"I am talking of someone—and while doing so, the time to smell roses… to fall in love with a white-gloved acrobat—dead since the beginning of time, that is fixed, for I refuse to live for any other end than the very one which I found to contain the first misfortune: that my life must be a legend, in other words, legible, and the reading of it must give birth to a certain new emotion which I call poetry. I am no longer anything, only a pretext."

"Ah, but Bunnie I loved you"

Missy. Missy. Missy.

Wait. You cancelled her because she wore a button?

O, darlins Missy Madonna and Me are the same age.

Rock stars, punks. His Purpleness.

It's called banging for a reason.

You expect us to be on the same page at the same time because you just decided what belongs on that page?

I am hated for loving.

I'm forced to ask: does this person want me/us dead?

Will they come to my rescue? Slay [for] me? The sword of no shit.

I've always welcomed a learning curve, a tossed line, sweet cream.

Morrissey. I've never expected him to be other than. An idol. Crooner. Rock god.

And wrong. Fuck, please allow me the space to get it wrong.

David Suzuki tells us, "It's too late" (baby, now, it's too late though we really did try to make it)

"For me, what we've got to do now is hunker down."

David Suzuki.

I haven't heard a death knell as certain since Jane Jacobs's *Dark Age Ahead.*

(Jacobs 2004. Suzuki 2025.)

Read it then. Saw it then.

Know it now.

Knew it hearing James Baldwin: "the world is held together by the love and the passion of a very few people."

Jimmy, smiling, chuckling with a draft and a smoke at a pub in Bowling Green, Ohio.

Baldwin didn't have a lived day not knowing. You? Same. Still, they wrote. Why?

Why (I mean thank you, but) Why? Why do anything?

"Hunker down kids!"

Because this fairy is a Fucking Taurus Romantic Moo-Cow Bitch.

I want a say in how and when I'm making my grand fucking exit.

If I were George Clooney, I would've deep kissed Mark Wahlberg at the end of *The Perfect Storm*.

Roseanne Barr did the funniest stand up I've ever seen in my life. Cowboy boots, hat and sparklers grinding to the Star-Spangled Banner.

So she went batshit crazy. She's got a right. I hope she drone explodes into a fucking zillion fireworks in the sky.

Who doesn't want to go out with a bang?!

And that's what really really pisses me off about our current Four Horsemen of the Apocalypse…

They see no one. Not even themselves.

No attention. Not a care.

Stone cold criminals.

"You don't think we do the same thing? They do to us… we do to them?"

Only with a bigger stick. God on our side.

Blood to the knees drill baby drill alligator alley gulf of america clubbing real estate branding wannabes with a smattering of rapture hungry true believers.

How many lives to be enrapt?

How many snuffed out in an instant this minute?

Darlins we all know the answer to that too.

This revolution will not be televised.

Free Palestine. Protect Trans Kids. Black Lives Matter. Land back. Climate Change Is Real.

Last dance. Last chance for love.

Hands Off My Body. Equal pay. Housing is a Right.
Give peace a

last chance for romance, tonight

the world without us. Glory be.

Dance me to the end of love.

May I have this dance?

Debwewin (Truth)

It's Sunday. 11°. Classic Toronto blue skies. My balcony door is open as I look across the street. Stop.

Gimme a minute… I'm simply taking in exactly what it is I'm seeing here.

The west side of a red brick school gym/auditorium, two of the four exit doors painted in rainbow stripes, red, orange, yellow, green, blue, purple, both with a sequence of five heart-shaped colours: black, brown, babyblue, pink, and white on each.

Between these exits there are three sections, each with placards of words both in Ojibway and English:

HONESTY / Gwayakwaadiziwin
WISDOM / Nbwaakaawin
LOVE / Zaagi'idiwin
RESPECT / Mnaadendmowin
HUMILITY / Zaagi'idiwin
BRAVERY / Aakode'ewin
TRUTH / Debwewin.

What a sight. Words to actions to practice, refine, live by. All the colours at play. Right here, in front of me. Remind/welcome me daily.

I face my immediate neighbour, Church Street Junior

Public School. Those are the doors I use to cast my vote with Elections Canada, and I've seen its growth from a single-level smallish JK-6 to a two-story extension with a winning new playground the kids take to regardless of the weather. It's a space where they hold 'family-friendly' activities over Pride, where the flag twirlers practice their parade routine and I still remember those doors opening to summer nights where gay couples and friends met to square dance weekly.

As described on their TDSB page, "Church St. P.S. has been part of the community (one of the most diverse in the city—and one of the friendliest) for almost 150 years, just north of Church and Carlton… fully accessible, the gateway to the 'village' and proud home of the Native Learning Centre." Two flags, Canadian and Pride, flap in the wind.

Along with the chicly modernized user-friendly playground, a dynamic new fence was erected that lights the entire strip of sidewalk, changing colours as pedestrians pass each other, kinda reminding me of the gorgeous colourbleeds during the title sequence of the film *Punch Drunk Love* with the fence primarily featuring Trans blues and pinks.

Children and their parents/caretakers, workers cross the rainbow crosswalk on the north corner (Church and Alexander), and a trans flag crosswalk south at Wood Street, where my co-op currently has this fun/cheesy Instagram moment welcome sign lit ("Valentine's?" "Love is Love?").

Then, before dawn, an explosion quakes my bed, windows blown out, our building's whooping crane alarm sounding off, I choke back smoke… see blue and red flashes across my bedroom ceiling, shouts from the pavement, a strange orange glow just off the balcony, more fire engines arriving, the entire school has been bombed, incinerated in flames, I look to the skies, low flying planes, paratroopers in clusters drop out of the clouds of billowing smoke… my hand touches my face, yes, it's mine…

I wake. A puddle of sweat.

Wiped out in an instant.

"President Donald Trump on Saturday denied U.S. involvement in a strike that killed more than 165 people at a girls' elementary school in Southern Iran, instead placing the blame on Iran.

When asked aboard Air Force One Saturday whether the U.S. conducted the February 28 strike, Trump said, without evidence, "No, in my opinion, based on what I've seen, that was done by Iran."

Buckets of rainbows over buckets of blood. Now and forever.

She will never bitch about "yet another rainbow" ever again. Ever.

Debwewin.

We Never Learn From History

There is no making it

better. Reparations. Justice.

The harm is done.

Infinitely. Repeatedly. Done.

Read history, the story that

you dropped in on is never

the story you want let alone

true. I guess that's called

childhood. The place of dreams.

Cinderella. Fairyland. The woods.

Each, a secret place

the place where they

can be (Crick? Tree?

Sky? Moss? Hollow?)

Nobody wanted this

history. The conquerors

and we but minions

Lovely creatures we are

I see you

Fairy

gigglepuss sparkle pony

turtle on a rock

chaser of grasshoppers

lightning bugs   Keeper

of the Bug Jar   entranced

by dancing waters

mistaking rabbit turds

for M&Ms   Tying your shoes

using bunny ears

Being the fastest joy

down the slope in Ottawa

Park fairy boy

of breezes

car windows down

she'd hang out

all the way if she could

Wanting it all   all of it

the swoop of telephone wires pass

their favourite drive-in marquee

Jesse James on a leaping horse

rootin' tootin' guns a-blazing into the sky

Pass the Adult Bookshop she bought

their first gay porn mag at

(walked all the way there and back)

Their first cock, a neighbour boy

"Mine's a German cock!," he smiles.

Typing my first love letter

on an IBM Selectric in HS

"I think you're the most beautiful boy in school."

Fairy, "What do you want, Girl?"

"I'm a boy, too." On the wrestling team,

managing track and field just to be near them

Getting high on spirits poppers

The best lubricants to enter

the temple of men. RUSH

A crush straddles my chest grabs my curls

holds me inches away, the blonde hairs

on his forearm "is this what you want?"

"All. I want all of it. My all. Your all."

Bars closed. Finally, the guts to show up at his door

only to puke in his bathtub.

Him. Holding my head.

Yet to believe, know I could actually be

"Say it, Kirby."

His hand holding my head

"I've said it."

"No," you said.

"I finally had the guts."

"You've always had the guts child. Suzanne saw to that."

"Then what? Fuck off."

"I want to be me. In this world. Free. Now."

"Girl. Are you fucking serious? For real?"

"Where/who do you think you've been all this time. MF?"

"No. It can't be that easy."

"Girl, EASY? E A S Y?!!! there ain't no

easy breezy cover girl easy… HELLO?

Simple, yes. Easy, no"

"But, go ahead, make it as tough as I know you like it."

"Fuck you Fairy."

"Child, I never thought you'd ask."

I want to be free of them.

Those who wish me dead.

"You didn't wish anyone dead?"

Not enough to buy an AK-17. Make it a law.

Fair.

Fuck fair.

"Call me Fairy."

No, I'm good, what I really want is no harm to come to anyone, I want to stop the suffering, spare others what we faced.

"Honey. You do that everyday getting up in the morning."

"I wish it didn't take money to do things."

"You've done all that shit without money honey."

"Yeah, but not a NYC apartment with a fire escape lit by neon."

"No, girl. A whole fucking life with little to no money."

"AND YOU WENT TO NEW YORK. SMOKED-UP WITH YOUR BEST FRIEND PAUL ON HIS FIRE ESCAPE NEW YEAR'S EVE NEAR THE CLOISTERS ON THE CORNER OF SEAMEN AND COMINGS AND MADE IT PRETTY."

With a smile and a flip-flop dance.

"Lambykins, you've been the very best free bouquet of lilies of the valley."

Here. Picked fresh today. Smell them.

O, the breeze.

I've never entered a relationship

believing I could be loved.

Does anyone?

Prove me wrong.

A grand few of you did.

Loved me, and I you.

My whole body gives thanks.

I do know what I want.

Nods to Sinead,

my life knows, too.

Only the moment, baby

the luck to have

this moment. Livable.

Bearable. Breathable.

Just this moment

joy in my belly

stinking of you.

To Kathryn Mocker

Let's have a gay moment, shall we?

I've never ever hated being a fag,

ever.

I fucking love it. Every pore molecule of my being

GAY gay.

O, sure, I've hated myself a-plenty

but never enough to not want to be homosexual.

I loved being homosexual.

"Don't give up on this plant."

A cutting from what I thought was an asparagus fern from her foyer. Wild wispy feathery fronds. Phyllis Diller hair.

Made it home. Potted. Placed it on the balcony.

Didn't "do" much (growth-wise?) always looking a bit scraggly, could never figure out if it was happy or not.

I asked her, showing her on her last visit.

"It's fine. Don't give up on this plant."

Good thing I brought them in yesterday clearing the balcony for winter.

Covered the AC. Pruned the mama crown of thorns.

"Suzy-Q. What am I to do with you?"

Looking at what I thought were idk—on closer inspection, blooms! Tiny.

Delicate.

Acknowledgements

"Bathhouse mazes…" first appeared in *Extrins: 13 Responses by poets of note to Kevin Strebner's* Inherent.

"Frociaggine" first appeared in *MiddleLost 4,* Winter 2025.

"I Want To Be a Faggot When I Grow Up" and "Simple Enough" first appeared in the chapbook *Simple Enough* (1985).

"Adam's Feet" first appeared in the chapbook *She's Having a Doris Day* (Knife | Fork | Book, 2017).

"Cockaholic" first appeared in the anthology *Queer View Mirror* (Arsenal Pulp Pres, 1995).

"The Battle of the Flesh," "Body Positive," and "Bob Smith Sucks Cock" first appeared in the chapbook *Cock & Soul* (Gay Vision Press, 1991).

"Spew" first appeared in *OUT Magazine* (Canada) circa 1995.

"The Good," "The Ripple in Your Flag," "Hello Stranger," "Are All Booksellers Dreamers?" "Floundering (Not Dead)," "How to Get Published," "How to Support Yourself as an Artist," "How I Loved Your Love," "Spill the T," "Do Your Homework," "Ah, but Bunnie I Loved You," "Debwewin (Truth)" first appeared at *Send My Love to Anyone.*

I wish to acknowledge the generous support of the Ontario Arts Council Recommender Grant Program, with special thanks to publisher Aimee Parent Dunn at Palimpsest Press and editor Jim Johnstone "the man who walks with me."

To Erín Moure, Neil Surkan, Klara du Plessis, Jessica Hiemstra, Ian Indiano, R. Kolewe, Norma Cole, Lisa Fishman, and Barbara Tran for their early reads and steadfast encouragement.

To loved ones, mostly named in this book, (some unnamed), faces, accurate reflectors dear to me. What keeps me here.

And, to my sidekick Kathryn Mockler at *Send My Love to Anyone*, she bows.

PHOTO: IAN INDIANO

KIRBY is the author of *She* (KFB, 2024), *Poetry is Queer* (Palimpsest Press, 2021), *This Is Where I Get Off* (Permanent Sleep Press, 2019), featured columnist at *Send My Love to Anyone*, and publisher at Knife | Fork | Book. kirbyfairy.ca